MOVE ON DOWN TO MEXICO 2024

Everything You Need to Know to Get Yourself Started Up and Settled In

Nicholas Grant

The Renegade Camellia Press

All photos by: Nicholas Grant

To Marie,
my wife and fellow adventurer

CONTENTS

INTRODUCTION

As you have probably already discovered, there are quite a few offerings in the move-to-Mexico book category, and each of them is geared to one audience or another or a particular area of focus. When I started writing this book, I had intended it to be a guide for those of limited retirement income who wanted to start a new and exciting life in Mexico rather than try making it back home eating instant ramen and canned sardines, to state things a bit overdramatically. I suppose you might say that was the sort of situation I was afraid of someday facing myself in life, and Mexico fit the bill just perfectly as a preferable and very doable solution. And so, I decided to go down for a year or two to check it out.

Being a bit of a neurotic, I overdid it a tad on the research side of things, and being the way I am, I kept notes at every step of the way, not only in regard to getting my visa, but for everything that I did or wanted to know how to do down there. I had amassed so much information that it could all fill a book, which is no doubt why my soon-to-be wife told me that I should turn it all into a book and publish it so as not to let it all go to waste, and that is how it came to pass that you are sitting there reading these words now.

Little by little things got a lot more expensive down in Mexico, particularly in regard to qualifying for residency, and I kept up with all that with great interest and, I admit, a bit of sadness, knowing that people who would really have benefited by a happy retirement alternative south of the border were being unintentionally priced out. And thus my initial vision of a book specifically geared to those sorts had to be abandoned.

What I have tried to do, however, is to keep things real by being as frank and honest as possible, and by trying to put out as much useful information as possible, information that should prove of use to a tourist, short-term resident, digital nomad, retiree, or anyone else who wants to have a taste of the Mexico experience.

Being honest and real means that I try to stick to what I know and not fudge the rest. Want to know about buying a beachfront condo and the legal and banking requirements to do so? Sorry, can't help you. Want to know about buying a house somewhere and renting it out as an AirBnB? Again, sorry, but that is way out of my field of expertise. I would be doing you a disservice by trying to fake my way through explaining that to you.

As for the setup of the book itself, I have tried to organize it for those want to get down to the details without having to wade through a pool of text. That means shorter, topically-focused chapters, with more cumbersome areas of concern, such as the visa acquisition process, broken down into separate chapters for each phase of that process. Basically, if I did things right, you should be able to know where to go in the book by looking at the Table of Contents alone. Fingers crossed I did a good job in that regard.

Although in the initial chapters I focus on visa and entry matters, since I am assuming that those who are the likely readers of this book want to get to that information as quickly and easily as possible, in the later chapters I have also provided some basic information related to living and/or travelling in Mexico that should be of use or interest to prospective future residents and visitors alike.

I should also mention that I have tried to keep the information in this book relevant to all parts of Mexico, and as far as visa and entry requirements, that holds true. As for feet-on-the-ground information though, I will obviously have more to say about those areas that I have lived in, been in, visited, or otherwise know the most about, which means that I will be more focused, or least more verbose, when discussing the colonial highlands than beach resorts.

In regard to the conventions used in this book, I have tried to keep things simple. I use the term *expat* for non-citizen foreigners, and I use the word *American* to refer to citizens of the United States. There are those expats in Mexico who take umbrage at the use of those terms, but my job is to make it clear who I am talking about in the shortest and clearest way possible. Anyway, I tend to think that those who are bothered by such terms misunderstand, or forget, those words' origins and the universality of their use outside the Mexican context. It's all up to you which terms you choose to use in your day-to-day dealings.

When it comes to the numbers used in this book, all are based on the information available to the public as of January 6, 2024. That means the amounts required in order to qualify for residency are valid until January 1 of the following year. As for exchange rates, well, those change hour by hour, so it would be impossible to try to keep such information completely up to date to the last minute. Instead, I use a rate of 17.03 pesos to the US dollar, which was a pretty average rate for the first week of the year.

Finally, I should note that the costs of things are always

changing, even in Mexico, so although the important numbers should be correct as of this writing, other costs are subject to inflation and thus should be considered in that vein.

That all said, happy reading, happy exploring! Enjoy the journey!

CHAPTER 1: REALITY CHECK

I hate to start my book off with a bit of a downer for an opener, but I think it behooves us all to make some things clear about Mexico as a place for retirement or long-term living. I see a lot of people who post in online groups that they want to move on down to Mexico with their family and start a new life. They speak decent Spanish and have some experience in this or that line of work and want to know what kind of jobs they can get. Uh oh.

Well, not so fast there. You can't just say, hey, I'm moving to Mexico, go down, find an apartment, land a job, and live happily ever after. Mexico doesn't have "open borders." No country does. No, to go to Mexico, either as a tourist or student or resident, you have to enter the country legally with the proper visa and, for work, permission. For purposes of tourism, entering Mexico legally is hard not to do, particularly for citizens of the US, Canada, and many other countries, but if you are on staying long term, then you need a residency visa, and that is where the problems begin for some.

While it is still true that you can live in Mexico fairly reasonably on a limited income, as you will soon discover in the next chapter, getting residency in Mexico requires proof of financial solvency, and what they want to see in terms of either income or savings is not what a person of limited income would consider limited. In order words, nowadays you need money to go down to Mexico and save money.

Ah, but I'll just go down on a tourist visa, do a border run when it expires, and get a new visa when I reenter the country, you say. Well, maybe you could get away with that a few years ago, but nowadays your comings and goings are digitally recorded, so the government will soon be wise to your attempting to circumvent the system, and since they are trying crack down on this, you could possibly be denied reentry or given a very limited period of time on reentry. And remember, they do arrest and deport visa violators in Mexico, so don't hang your hopes on what is now bad advice from former successful practitioners of the art.

And that brings us to the topic of working in Mexico. A lot of folks see immigrants from Mexico or other countries come to the US, get jobs, and do well for themselves in their new lives. Seeing this, they think they'll do the same thing, just in the opposite direction. Well, it works for those who come up because wages and job opportunities north of the border are far greater than they are south of it. If you are going the other way round, i.e., south, then you have to expect fewer jobs, longer hours, and much lower wages, none of which is exactly what you are mostly likely hoping to hear. On top of that you are not allowed to work in Mexico unless you are granted a visa that permits you to work.

Permanent Residency is one of them, but it requires a lot of money for proof of solvency, either in income or savings, and these days it is only being granted at consulates abroad to retirees. You can get permission to work as a *Visitor with permission to conduct remunerated activities*, but that requires first being hired by a Mexican company, and the chances of that are fairly slim unless you have excellent Spanish skills and an expertise in some area that is insufficiently covered in Mexico. In other words, OXXO is not going to hire you to work as a cashier in one of their convenience stores, and the government would most likely deny your application for work permission if they did.

It is possible that you could land a job from your home country to work for a branch office in Mexico for a limited period of time, as is often the case for certain employees of, for example, the foreign automobile makers, or of course, but it is more likely that if you got hired by anyone, it would be by a school to teach English, but again at lower wages and longer hours than you would like.

No, most expats who work in Mexico do so as digital nomads, working online for companies that are located and/or providing services generating income from abroad. That is the safest route if working is on your mind, and it is no doubt the most lucrative.

Again, it is not my intention to dash people's hopes and dreams in the first few pages of my book, but I also don't want you to harbor false hopes and get yourself into a bind based on misunderstanding the reality landscape and/or being urged on by you-can-do-it-if-you-really-want-to hyper-optimists, who are always there while you are planning and dreaming but never around when things don't work out as promised.

No, Mexico is indeed a great place, and if you can move there, you are sure to like it, even if living there long term is not what you end up doing. So, by all means, read on through the book, and see what it takes to move on down and what awaits you once you're there. At any rate, the quest itself often reveals new avenues you might not have considered before. Hopefully it will lead you where you'd like to be!

CHAPTER 2: RESIDENCY OVERVIEW

Temporary and Permanent Residency

Rather than start things off by talking about visiting Mexico as a tourist, let's jump straight into the stuff that I would think most of you want to know about - how to live legally in Mexico long term. If living in Mexico long-term is indeed your plan, then you need to get a residency visa, and there are two main categories of these: Temporary Residency and Permanent Residency. These visas must be applied for outside of Mexico at a Mexican consulate. You cannot apply for either within Mexico except in certain very specific cases, such as marriage to a Mexican national.

Temporary Residency

Temporary Residency, or *Residencia Temporal*, is the easier of the two visa types to get, and it has some other advantages too. The most important of these is that you need less money to qualify for temporary residency. On top of that, the actual fees you must pay for the visa are lower, at least initially. For those planning or hoping to bring their car down to Mexico with them, the *Temporal* allows you to do so without having to go through the cumbersome and costly *nationalization* process. In fact, many aspiring expats who qualify for permanent residency, opt to instead apply for the *Temporal* for this very reason. Ah, but more on the topic of cars in a later chapter.

The main disadvantage of the *Residente Temporal* is that you cannot work on that visa, at least not for an employer that is paying you in Mexico. You can work online with the Temporal, as long as the employer is not in Mexico and the actual payments are coming from abroad.

Some worry that the *Residente Temporal* is a dead-end street. After all, why would you want temporary residency if you plan to stay in Mexico for the rest of your life, right? Well, that line of thinking is actually faulty because the Temporal is not a dead-end street at all. It is granted for one year, and after that, you can extend it within Mexico for an additional three years for a total of four years. You can do this either in one-year increments or all three additional years at once.

The advantage to doing it all at once is that you don't have to go back to the local immigration office, better known locally as the *INM* (*Instituto Nacional de Migración*), every year. The disadvantage of doing it all at once is that you have to pay three years of fees up front, which can be rough for many people, but at least you have an option. The best thing of all, and the reason why going the Temporal route is not a dead end, is because after your four years of living as a *Residencia Temporal* holder is complete, you can convert your visa over to Permanent Residency without having to provide new financials. In other words, if you can't afford Permanent Residency when you first apply to move down, you'll be able to get it without problems a few years down the road - at least that is how the rules stand now in most states.

Permanent Residency

Permanent Residency, or *Residencia Permanente,* is what most people hope to get when they get the idea of moving to Mexico in mind. There are a couple good reasons to want it too, one of which is that you will not have to go to the immigration office (INM) ever again. An even bigger perk is that you are also eligible to work. In fact, you are pretty much allowed to do anything save for vote, participate in political demonstrations, and/or run for office. You have to be a citizen to do any of those things.

The main disadvantage of the *Permanente* is that qualifying for it requires much more money for proof of solvency. Also, as I mentioned in the previous section, you cannot bring in your car from back home without spending the money to nationalize it, assuming the car qualifies for that anyway.

What Are The Requirements?

Qualifying for either Temporary or Permanent Residency is all a question of money and how much of it you have. You can prove solvency in either of two ways - either by having a sufficient monthly income OR a sufficient amount of money in savings. You do not have to satisfy both. One is enough to do the trick.

The actual amounts of income or savings required are based on formulas that are tied to the Mexican minimum wage in Mexico City. Many complain that the numbers have no relation to the reality of the actual cost of living in Mexico, and they are correct. You can live in Mexico for far, far less than they require for proof of solvency, but for whatever reason, the requirements are what they are, and, well, below are the formulas that the qualification amounts are determined by.

For Temporary Residency (*Residente Temporal*), you must show proof of either:

A monthly income for the past six months equal to 300 X the daily minimum wage in Mexico City

OR

Savings or other fluid assets (IRAs, Mutual Funds, etc.) for the past 12 months equal to 5000 X the daily minimum wage in Mexico City

For Permanent Residency (*Residente Permanente*), you must show proof of either:

A monthly income for the past six months equal to 500 X the daily minimum wage in Mexico City

OR

Savings or other fluid assets (IRAs, Mutual Funds, etc.) for the past 12 months equal to 20,000 X the daily minimum wage in Mexico City

In case, you are wondering why the formula specifies the minimum wage in Mexico City, rather than in Mexico at large, it is because there are actually two different minimum wages in Mexico. That for Mexico City is the standard for most of the country, but there is also a slightly higher daily minimum wage for the northern border states, as people there have higher costs of living due to their distance from the rest of the country and having to deal more often with a more expensive northern neighbor. That said, consider yourself lucky that the formulas use the lower of the two figures.

Some people have complained about the amounts required to qualify for solvency, amounts that make it much harder (i.e., more expensive) for regular ol' expat retirees to qualify for residency. This they often attribute to new rules being at play, but that is not the case. The rules have not changed. The formulas have not changed. The only thing that has changed is the minimum wage. . . and that is what has made it more difficult for expats to qualify for residency in Mexico.

The minimum wage in 2016 was only 73 pesos a day, by 2018, the year I moved down, it was up to 88 pesos a day, which meant, for example, that I only had to show proof of about $1400 US income to get my temporary residency. But the increases kept on coming. In 2019 it increased 16%, in 2020 by 20%, and by 15% in 2021. At the start of 2022, it was up again by 23%, for 2023, 20%, and up another 20% again for 2024, bringing the current minimum wage for Mexico City to $248.93 MX. That is an increase of $41.49 MX from the year before! While all this is on the face of it great news for the Mexican worker, it means that things are tougher on the wannabe expats of more modest financial means.

To see how it all works out, using temporary residency as an example, take the current daily minimum wage for a worker in Mexico City, which is $248.93 MX and multiply that by 300, as specified in the formula. That means that you have to show a monthly income for the past six months of $74,679 MX, and when you walk into the Mexican consulate in the US, they are going to ask for an equivalent dollar amount, so take that amount, $74,670 MX, and divide it by the current exchange rate (which as of this writing is of $17.03 MX to the $1 US), and you will come up with the figure they will probably have in mind, in this case $4385 US. If you had applied just a few months ago when the exchange rate was M$19.60, the amount you'd have to show would only have been $3809 US! So as you can see, not only does the minimum wage have an effect on what you have to show the consulate to qualify, so does the Peso-to-Dollar exchange rate.

Can I Use Property To Prove Solvency?

The answer to this question is both *yes* and *no*, depending on what you mean. If you mean that you want to use the current market value of your equity in your home back home to show as assets to prove solvency, then the answer is *no*. Fluid assets in concrete numerical amounts is what the consulate will want to see from you.

If, however, you mean that you own a home in Mexico and want to use the value of that home to prove solvency, then, *yes... maybe*. You see, a home that you own in Mexico can be used for proof of solvency but only for Temporary Residency. On top of that, you must own the home free and clear (*i.e.,* no loans, no liens), and the value has to be at least the amount arrived at by the formula 40,000 X the minimum wage in Mexico City. That comes to almost $10,000,000 MX, which is about $588,000 US. I mean, if you were able to slam down that much on a house in Mexico, I doubt you're really going to be needing to worry about the other ways of qualifying for residency.

So Is There Any Way Around These High Qualification Amounts?

Basically, for most folks, not really, but if you happen to fall into one of the following categories, there is hope. These categories are:

- Having a Mexican national spouse.
- Having at least one parent who is a Mexican national.
- Having a child born in Mexico.

For those of you falling into one of the categories above, which are really beyond the scope of this book, you can contact a Mexican consulate in your home country and find out more. If you live in Mexico, you can do the same (and even apply) at an immigration office (INM) in Mexico.

If you are going to Mexico as a university student or as a hiree of a Mexican company, the requirements are different, and usually less stringent money-wise. Your future school or employer will be guiding you in these cases, but you can also find out more on requirements for either visa type on most Mexican consulate website.

Regularization

Finally there is one last hope for some of you if you meet the requirements, and that is through a program that was begun during the time of COVID called *regularization*. To qualify for residency under this program, you must currently be in Mexico with an expired tourist visa, and you must have proof of having been in Mexico prior to 2022. You then pay the INM some fees and then a fine for having overstayed your visa. The nice thing about this route is that you don't have to provide any financials to prove solvency and you get four years of residency right off the bat.

Unfortunately, the program is temporary and it is not available everywhere in Mexico. Beware of those know-it-all folks who you will run across on Facebook and other Mexico forums or groups who will push Regularization as the miracle cure for everyone's ills. It is, as I said, temporary, not available everywhere, and. . . the rules can vary from state to state where it is still available, so look into it, but don't get your hopes up too much until you are given reason by an INM office to do so.

UMA

More of a Hail Mary pass for hope than an actual way around qualifying for the high solvency requirements, at least at the present time, is the *UMA*. UMA (*Unidad de Medida y Actualización*) is an acronym you are likely to come across either in your investigations into moving to Mexico or, assuming you are successful in getting down there, once you are in Mexico. The UMA, which rather inelegantly translates to *Unit of Measure and Update*, is a figure that was created for governmental use to provide a more realistic cost-of-living figure for use in place of the minimum wage in various formulas used to determine fees and solvency qualifications within Mexico. While the daily minimum wage in Mexico as of January 1, 2024 is now up to

$248.93 MX, the UMA for 2024 is only $103.74 MX.

While it had been assumed when the UMA was established that it would be used not only domestically, but also at Mexican consulates abroad, that latter bit has yet to happen. Many expat wannabes hold out hope that this will someday come to pass, and with good reason. First of all, the UMA, when used instead of the minimum wage in solvency requirement formulas is a much better reflection of what it actually costs to live in Mexico. Second, the amounts required for proof of solvency would be considerably lower than they are now if the UMA were used instead of the Minimum Wage. For example, if the UMA were used instead of the minimum wage in the current solvency formula for Temporary Residency, you would only have to show proof of an income of $31,122 MX (about $1827 US) a month rather than the current $74,679 MX ($4394 US) required in the minimum-wage based formula. For the savings amount, it would be only $518,700 MX (about $30,458 US) in the UMA-based formula compared to the $1,244,650 MX ($73,085 US) required per the minimum wage based formula. As you can see, that is a very big difference.

Alas, there have been no signs thus far that the consulates are planning to adopt the UMA for their purposes. Nevertheless, it is one ray of hope that you might look out for if things look bleak for now. If nothing else, the UMA is used domestically in Mexico, so if you do manage to move down and for some reason are required to prove solvency in Mexico at some point in the future for some yet unforeseen reason, at least you can feel a bit better knowing that the figures will be UMA rather than minimum wage based.

Digital Nomad And Retirement Visas?

Before wrapping up this chapter, I thought I should clearly and emphatically state three things that people seem to repeatedly, but understandably, get wrong:

1. Mexico has no visa called a *Digital Nomad Visa!*
2. Mexico has no visa called a *Retirement Visa*!
3. Mexico has no visa called a *Pensionado Visa!*

While some countries might have visas that go by those names, Mexico does not. While you can go to Mexico and be a digital nomad, there is no visa specifically by that name or specifically geared toward that purpose. Why? Because it is not necessary. Those who want to go to Mexico as digital nomads can just go as tourists, for short terms experiences, or apply for temporary residency for longer term experiences.

Many people incorrectly call the Permanent Residency visa the *Retirement Visa*. This is an understandable error because many Mexican consulates will only issue Permanent Residency visas to retirees. Still, there are two problems with that naming: 1) *Retirement Visa* is not the correct name of the visa, and 2) it is not only issued to those who have retired. For example, if you go to Mexico on a Temporary Residency visa before you have retired, you would qualify for Permanent Residency in Mexico after four years, whether you had since retired or not.

As for the *Pensionado Visa*, such is the name of the visa that is issued to retirees in many other Latin American countries. Costa Rica, Nicaragua, and Ecuador, for example, all offer Pensionado visas for foreign retirees, but Mexico does not have anything by that name. In Mexico, you either apply for a Temporary Residency visa or a Permanent Residency visa if you want to retire there.

CHAPTER 3: RESIDENCY AS A FAMILY UNIT

If you are single and/or going to Mexico solo, then there is no need for you to read this chapter other than to satisfy your curiosity. If, however, you are planning on heading down to Mexico with your spouse or your minor child, or both, then this section will prove to be of great use for you. You see, if you are moving to Mexico as a family, you can apply for residency as a family unit, either as a couple or as parent/s and child/ren.

This approach is a sort of perk for you, as only one person has to meet the full financial minimum for solvency. For each of the other *dependents*, only a smaller additional amount per person must be shown, and that amount is based on the formula: 100 X the daily minimum wage in Mexico City. Whether it be for Temporary or Permanent Residency, and whether you are using an income based or savings based approach to prove solvency, the formula for each dependent is the same: 100 X the minimum wage in Mexico City

To see this in play, let's use a couple, husband and wife, applying for Temporary Residency based on monthly income as an example (with 248.93 being the daily minimum wage) with Spouse 1 being the primary qualifying application and Spouse 2 being the dependent:

Spouse 1 @ 300 X $248.93 MX = $74,679 MX
Spouse 2 @ 100 X $248.94 MX = $24,893 MX
Total monthly income necessary = $99,572 MX

At today's exchange rate of $17 MX ($17.03, to be exact) to the USD, that comes to a monthly income of about $5,845.78 US! That's sure not cheap, but it's better than if each person tried to qualify for him/herself.

As I already noted, the amount required for the dependent is the same formula whether you are going for proof of solvency through income or through savings: 100 X Minimum Daily Wage in Mexico City. Thus the requirements for a couple using the twelve-months-of-savings route to prove solvency would be:

Spouse 1 @ 5000 X $248.93 MX = $1,244,650 MX
Spouse 2 @ 100 X $248.94 MX = $24,893 MX
Total amount of savings necessary = $1,269,543 MX

Permanent Residency Via Family Unit

If you are wondering about applying for Permanent Residency via the Family Unit route, things work in the same way. The qualifying spouse must meet the minimum amount required per the 500 X Minimum Wage formula, if qualifying based on income, or 20,000 X Minimum Wage, if qualifying based on savings. And yet for the dependent, the amount of additional income or additional savings required is the same as for monthly income: 100 X Minimum Wage. You can see it play out in the numbers. First taking a look at those for Permanent

Residency based on monthly income:

Spouse 1 @ 500 X 248.93 MX = $124,470 MX
Spouse 2 @100 X $248.94 MX = $24,893 MX
Total monthly income necessary = $149,363 MX

Again, coming to a whopping $8,769.91 US for the two, that is not cheap at all, but again much less than if each tried to qualify on his/her own. If you are going the savings route, the numbers would look like this:

Spouse 1 @ 20,000 X 248.93 MX = $4,978,600 MX
Spouse 2 @ 100 X $248.94 MX = $24,893 MX
Total amount of savings necessary = $5,003,493 MX

> **NOTE:** As you can see, the amount required for a dependent spouse is the same amount for both the Temporary and Permanent Residency categories. This points to one of the oddities of the Family Unit approach to applying for residency. While both husband and wife applying for Temporary Residency in this way will leave the office with Temporary Residency visas, a husband and wife applying for Permanent Residency in this manner, will not. Instead, the qualifying spouse will receive a Permanent Residency visa, while the dependent spouse will receive a Temporary Residency visa. Of course, after one year in Mexico, the dependent spouse will then renew his or her temporary visa, and then later switch over to Permanent Residency without need for further financials.

Dependent Children

Everything said thus far also holds true for minor children. That means that whichever visa you are applying for, the qualifying applicant must meet the full requirements, while for the dependent spouse and/or child only an additional 100 X the minimum wage in Mexico City per dependent must be shown. Thus, to give another example, if a husband and wife were planning on applying for Temporary Residency based on monthly income for themselves and their two minor children, they would have to show the following numbers for solvency:

Spouse 1 @ 300 X $248.93 MX = $74,679 MX
Spouse 2 @ 100 X $248.94 MX = $24,893 MX
Child 1 @ 100 X $248.94 MX = $24,893 MX
Child 2 @ 100 X $248.94 MX = $24.893 MX
Total monthly income for family of 4 = $149,358 MX

That comes to a monthly income of $8770 US. More than I've ever made in my life! Ouch! This is where qualifying by savings begins to make more sense, assuming you've got the savings, because the percentage of additional savings you need to show is less than the percentage of additional savings required. Take a look at the numbers:

Spouse 1 @ 5000 X $248.93 MX = $1,244,650 MX
Spouse 2 @ 100 X $248.94 MX = $24,893 MX
Child 1 @ 100 X $248.94 MX = $24,893 MX
Child 2 @ 100 X $248.94 MX = $24.893 MX
Total savings for family of 4 = $1,319,329 MX

The total savings required comes to a whopping $77,470 US, which is not exactly what everyone has lying around in their accounts, but it is a more likely savings amount than a $8770 US monthly income, at least for the common man.

I won't belabor the point by tossing in the figures for Permanent residency based on savings using this family-of-four scenario, but you now know what numbers to plug in and how to do the math to figure out what the amount necessary would be. You should note, however, that just as was the case for a dependent spouse qualifying via this avenue, the same is true for dependent children: only the qualifying applicant will get the Permanent Residency visa, while the dependent spouse and children will only get Temporary Residency at the time of application.

Additional Requirements For Family Unit Applications

If you are applying for residency using the Family Unit approach, note that you will need an official copy of your marriage certificate and official copies of your childrens' birth certificates. Some consulates will require that either one of these, or both, be apostilled, so be sure to check that out with the consulate you will be using when preparing your paperwork.

CHAPTER 4: APPLYING FOR RESIDENCY - PART 1

The Home Country Phase

Once you know which visa you want and think that you qualify for it, it is time to apply. That process involves a few rather simple steps that you can do quite easily on your own. You do not need to hire an attorney for this phase, as you will be gathering and submitting the documents to the consulate yourself anyway, and when it is time to go to the consulate, well, you have to go yourself. On top of that, staff at Mexican consulates in the United States are quite capable in English, so there is no language barrier to worry about.

Choosing Your Consulate And Making Your Appointment

The very first thing you will need to do is to decide which Mexican consulate you are going to use as this will affect exactly what documentation you will need to bring and what numbers you are going to have to show proof of. It is important to know that the solvency formulas are the official government guidelines. What the consulate you go to wants to see can vary quite a bit. This is due to how each consulate interprets the rules, when they update their requirement amounts, which exchange rate they choose to use, and so on.

As you will soon discover, consulates can vary greatly in what they ask for. For example, in October of 2023, I emailed five different consulates asking for their requirements for temporary residency, and the solvency amounts themselves were much more varied than I had expected. The figures were based on the 2023 minimum wage, but you can see how different they were from one another:

El Paso: $3,570
Tuscon: $3,300
Phoenix: $2,530
Nogales: $3,700
Las Vegas: $3,111

Not only did the amounts vary, but the documents required and the form they were wanted in also varied a great deal with some consulates being much fussier than others. It can also be rather confusing, a mystery really, to figure out what exchange rate a given consulate uses. Just this morning I got the new financial requirements for one consulate by email. The required amounts were given in dollars, and the dollar amounts seemed oddly high. Doing the math, it appeared that the particular consulate in question was using an exchange rate of $15.56 MX to the Dollar, which is the worst rate I've seen in a very long time, the worst of 2023 having been $16.68 on June 30. Anyway, the point here is that even the exchange rate used by one consulate can differ from another, and, of course, each one can update the rate they use at any time.

That all said, you will discover, and most who have gone through the process in borderline cases will agree, that it behooves you to shop around when it comes to consulates. The good thing is that, with a very few exceptions, you can pretty much go to any Mexican consulate in the country, no matter where you actually live, to apply for your visa. For example, I, a resident of North Carolina at the time, applied for my visa in Las Vegas, NV, and while there, I came upon a few other aspiring expats applying for their residency visas, one from Lubbock, TX, another from Seattle, WA, and yet another from Regina, Saskatchewan, Canada!

So, how do you actually go about choosing which consulate to use? Well, the best way is to first email two or three of the consulates geographically closest to you and ask for their requirements for temporary and permanent residency visas. They will usually get back to you by the end of the day or within a day or two at the most. Don't bother calling on the phone as a) you seldom get though, and b) you want their requirements in writing. Another good thing to do is to go to an Expats in Mexico type Facebook group and ask if anyone has had experience with the consulate you are considering going to. If you are warned away from any of your choices, ask for recommendations for others from the group (and ignore any of the snarky responders - Facebook is full of them), and/or write to a second tier of consulates, or those recommended in the online groups you asked, and see what they expect of you.

Once you have chosen your consulate, make an appointment with them according to the instructions provided in their email or the pdf they sent by email. This usually just consists of you emailing back and asking for an appointment. In some cases, they will ask you to email them pdfs of all the documents they ask for, and after they review them, they'll make an appointment for you. Pretty easy all in all.

Your Consulate Visit

What happens next after you've made your appointment depends on the consulate you are going to. The traditional and still most common route is as follows:

1. From that consulate's website, download, print, and fill out the Visa Application Form. (Many attach this application to the email they send you with their requirements). It is a simple form used for both the Temporal and Permanente visas. Bring this on the day of your appointment, along with all the items specified by your consulate. This will usually consist of:

a. Your passport and a photocopy of the information and photo page therein. Some also want copies of the pages with visas or entry and exit stamps on them.

b. One passport-size photo for the visa itself (this can be a different photo from that in your passport, but it should follow US Passport Agency guidelines). Some consulates will ask you to affix the photo to the visa application; others will not.

c. Copies or originals of the required number of bank statements. Check with the consulate to see what they will accept. Some consulates are much fussier than others. Some require originals and copies, while others will accept printouts of online statements. Whatever they ask for, bring extra photo copies in case they ask for them at the last minute. Keep these all organized so that you don't have to sort them out at the consulate.

d. You will also need to bring $51 application fee.

2. Once your docs are submitted at your appointment, the official at the consulate will ask you a few simple questions, including where you plan to live in Mexico, so be prepared to answer that, even if you are not sure it will be your long-term home. They are not going to throw you any gotcha questions, so don't be worried. And don't talk about working in Mexico, even if it is virtually. Nothing raises suspicions and worries of immigration gatekeepers who hear the word "work."

3. You will then be photographed and fingerprinted, and then, depending on the location, you will be told to come back in a couple hours to pick up your visa. At others you might be asked to come back a few days later to pick it up.

And that is basically that. Once you get your passport back, you will find your visa on one of its pages. The visa stamp is actually more of a full-page permanently attached sticker that has all your information, your photo, and the visa type on it. It alone, however, is really nothing more than a visa pre-approval. You do not really have residency yet. Not until you have entered Mexico, done what you have to do at the immigration office (INM) there, and received your residency card will you be legal. But the hard part is over. The easier but slightly fussier part is next to come...

Warning! The Clock Is Now Ticking!

From the day you receive that visa pre-approval stamp in your passport, you are on a timeclock. You now have six months in which to move to Mexico. Not to pop down to Mexico for a day or two. No, six months in which to move. You could move on down the very next day, or you could move down on the 179th day, as long as you get down there before six months, or 180 days, is up, you are good to go.

NOTE: It is very important to remember that once you

have that visa pre-approval stamp in your passport, you have only one option when it comes to going to Mexico, and that is moving down to complete the process at the INM office closest to where you will be living. No longer can you just pop across the border for lunch or for a weekend at the beach. You cannot go down for a couple of weeks to scout out a place to live either.

"But, oh, my best friend is doing a location wedding in Puerto Vallarta next month, and I can't move on down until a couple months later. But I have to go to the wedding!"

Well, no, you don't. You should have applied for your visa after the wedding. Tough luck it is, but those are the rules. No, now that you have that visa stamp in your passport, you have to be going down to stay. . . or at least be prepared to hang for a while until you get that residency card!

If you go in as a tourist while that visa stamp is in your passport and you do not yet have a residency card, then your residency will be void, and you will have to go back to square one - back to the consulate, paying another $51, and applying again.

That all said, get your tourism, housing scouting, and destination wedding attending out of the way BEFORE you apply for your visa at a consulate in your own country.

CHAPTER 5: APPLYING FOR RESIDENCY - PART 2

The Mexico, or Canje, Phase

So now that you have that residency pre-approval stamp in your passport, have your bags packed, and are on your way, it is important to know what awaits you. And what awaits you is the most important part of the process because once it is done, you are a legal resident of Mexico. Until then, you are not. In fact, if you don't go through with the in-Mexico part of the process, you will be, after 30 days, illegal within the country, so all your trying to do things by the book will have been for naught.

As I mentioned at the end of the previous chapter, the most important thing to do once you get that visa stamp affixed within your passport is to move down to Mexico within 180 days, and once you are in Mexico, you must move on to the second phase of your visa quest, often called the *Canje* phase.

Canje

Many soon-to-be permanent or temporary residents are surprised and a bit confused when they first enter Mexico and are only granted a 30-day stay by the passport control official. To many folks that seems like a mistake. "Surely something is wrong," the thinking goes," I have a permanent residency visa in my passport!"

Yes, it might seem like a mistake, but it is in fact totally correct, so don't worry. In fact, if that official gives you any number of days less than or more than 30. . . well, that is when you need to worry!

You see, at this point you are not a resident yet. You have been pre-approved for residency by a Mexican consulate back home, and you have legally entered Mexico, and have thus been entered into the system. You still have one more step to go, however, before you are actually an official resident of Mexico. . . and you only have 30 days in which to do it.

For this second phase of the residency acquisition process you must get yourself to the local immigration office. The immigration offices, known as INM, or *Instituto Nacional de Migración*, are usually, but not always, in the capital of each Mexican state, and there are sometimes offices in other locations that have a lot of expats or other non-citizens. You can see a list of offices with addresses, phone numbers and hours at the link below.

https://www.gob.mx/inm/acciones-y-programas/horario-y-oficinas-del-inm

On that page, just click on the name of the state where you will be living or staying when completing the process.

This is what is known as the *Canje* (Spanish for *exchange*) phase of the process, a phase that will complete the visa acquisition process, and you will know that the phase, and thus entire process, is complete when you have been handed your residency card. The fact that the card is green is why some expats call it the Mexican "green card," though it is not the really the same thing as the US card going by the same nickname, which is not even green anymore.

First Things First - Getting Through Passport Control Correctly

So once again, you are on a timeclock, this time a 30-day one, but before you can get on to your INM office to start the part-two ball rolling, you need to make sure you get through passport control correctly.

"Correctly" might sound an odd word to use here, but it is appropriate. The vast majority of people entering Mexico each day are either Mexican citizens or foreign tourists, not people coming to start a new life on as temporary or permanent residents. That being the case, it is very easy for you, as a non-citizen, to get processed almost automatically, albeit incorrectly, as a tourist. Don't let that happen! And the onus of preventing that from happening is on you!

So how do you prevent that from happening? Well, here are some basic pointers that should get the job done:

- Do not go or be guided through any sort of electronic or mechanical passport recording or processing device. You want to be handled by a real person. If there is an officer or other personnel there at the airport pointing you to such a device, show them the visa page of your passport and say or ask "canje." (If you can speak Spanish, you can, of course, of course, be more loquacious in saying this).

- If you are in the line of real passport control person, hand him/her the passport open to the visa page and say "canje."

Entering Correctly Via A Land Border

If you are entering Mexico via a land border by car or even on foot, remember that at most land crossings you will not go through passport control as a matter of course. You are often just essentially waved in, and no one will tell you that you need to go through passport control. You'd be surprised how many people find themselves in a bit of a mess because they cross without anyone checking their passport and thus assume, because no official said otherwise, it must be OK.

No, it is not OK, especially for anyone going outside the confines of that border town on the Mexican side of the crossing, and it is especially not OK for anyone with a residency visa. Therefore, it is your responsibility once across to stop at the immigration office (INM) on the Mexican side of the border complex to get your entry recorded.

All border crossings have such an office, though some are only open during daylight working hours, so please check the offices hours before you go. Such land crossings usually require you to fill out an FMM card, and if they do, make sure that the agent there understands that you are entering as a resident-to-be by presenting him/her with your passport open to the visa page and saying "canje."

Your Visit To The INM

To be admittedly repetitious to the point of being downright annoying, I will once again say that now that you are in the country, you have 30 and only 30 days to get to the INM office. I would not wait that long though. Things can go wrong, holidays might come up that you aren't aware of, and thus you could find your local INM office closed for more days than you imagined possible. Or, you might go to the office only to find that they only do business with those who have a reservation, and. . .well, anything can happen. That said, aim to go early - like no later than one week after arrival.

It is worth mentioning at this point that many people opt to use the services of a professional immigration facilitator or attorney for this phase of the process. People have different reasons for using a facilitator, and a big one is language, since many of the INM offices have no English-speaking workers. Because of the language issue and because of the fact that some offices can be very fussy about things, a facilitator, well familiar with the quirks and requirements at the local office/s they service, can be of great help.

Other people, of course, do it all on their own, either having sufficient Spanish ability for the job, a Spanish-speaking acquaintance willing to help them out and go to the office with them, or because they happen to know that the office they will be using has one or more English-speaking workers. The only way to determine the last point is to ask around in advance, either at the INM office itself, or in an online group for your area where fellow expats will most likely know from experience.

If you plan to go about doing this phase on your own, either completely solo or with someone to help you out for translation purposes, you will first need to find out whether or not your office requires you to have an appointment. You can call your local office to check or ask around in a local FB group to see what the case might be. Either way, when you do go, appointment or not, be sure to get there early as there can be fairly big lines at some offices.

The INM will either email you a list of things that you will need to bring, or they will send you a link to the government website that lists what you need to bring to your first visit to the INM office. That government website is useful because it not only lists what you need to bring, but it also has links to any forms you need to fill out. You can reach that website by going to the following URL:

https://www.inm.gob.mx/mpublic/publico/inm-tramites.html

Once the page above opens, click the **Trámites Migratorios** button, and then on the next page that opens, click the **Expedición de documento migratorio por canje** button

The site itself is auto-translated, so it should be easy enough to follow. To give you an preview of what is listed there, here is a brief rundown of the things you will need to bring to the INM office:

- A copy of the application that you fill out online. (You only have to provide answers for those questions that have an asterisk above them).

- Proof of your payment for the visa: $5108 MXN (Temporary Resident for one year) or $6226 MXN (Permanent Resident). This must be paid before you go to the INM office but after you have filled out the application listed above. There is actually a form on the site in the Payment section that you fill out, print out, and then take to the bank along with your passport.

- Your actual passport and a copy of it (The government page does not specify what exactly to copy, but in both my wife's and my own they just wanted a copy of the information/photo page. You might want to confirm this point with your INM office).

- Your actual residency visa (which the Mexican consulate back home affixed within your passport), and a copy of it.

- Your actual FMM card and a copy of it. Since all airports and now some land crossings are using FMMds instead of the long paper card, provide a copy of that FMMd stamp in your passport, the one that says "canje."

- You will also be providing 3 small "card size" photos. In the past, you would have to go to a professional photographer and have these taken, but now the photos are taken at the INM office, which is a good thing because they were so fussy about all aspects of these photos.

Once you have all your docs and copies and go to the INM office, your paperwork will be reviewed, and assuming all is hunky dory with all that, they will take your photos, fingerprint you, and have you fill out a few more things. When that is all done, what happens next depends on the office where you apply. At some, you might receive your resident card that same day, while at others, you might simply be sent an email with a number and password to use when checking in with their online portal to see when your cards are ready. They will give you some sort of time frame in which that will happen, and usually it is not that long.

Sometimes, however, weird things can happen and the process can take much longer than anticipated. In my own case, I had to wait about a month for my card because there was a shortage of card printing blanks. Machines can also break down or run out of ink or. . . well, anything. That all said, don't be planning to head out of the country the day after your INM office visit. Bureaucracy is what it is, and it can be slow.

The good news is that once you do have that card in hand, you are a resident!! The worry is over.

NOTE: Speaking of worrying, the 30-day countdown that I mentioned over and over earlier in the chapter is your deadline for *starting* the process with the INM. That does not mean that the INM has to complete your application in 30 days. It usually does, but, as I said, sometimes things happen, and you have to wait. Worry not, however, as you are completely legal as long as you have started the process.

CHAPTER 6: VISITING MEXICO AS A TOURIST

Well, now that I have covered all there is to cover about legal long-term residency in Mexico, since I am assuming that is what most people want to know right away, let's jump back a bit and look at the topic of just visiting Mexico as a tourist. Fortunately, going to Mexico as a tourist is quite easy for most of the intended readers of this book.

Do I Need A Passport To Visit Mexico?

Legally, *yes*. According to Mexican law, you need a passport or passport card to enter and be in Mexico. As to whether or not you can get away with not having a passport, it depends. If you are flying in, then definitely *no*. You won't even be allowed on the plane without one. If you are entering by car or on foot, then probably *yes*, since most likely no one will ask to look at any documentation from you when you enter the country. Having a passport or passport card will make your reentry into the US much faster and easier, though, so that is a good reason to have one with you in its own right.

> **NOTE:** If you have a US passport card, remember that you can only use it to enter by land or sea, although some websites will tell you, incorrectly, that you can use it for flying into Mexico as well.

Do I Need A Visa Just To Visit?

The answer for most folks is *no*. Basically, if you are a citizen of the USA, Canada, Japan, most EU countries, or some South and Central American countries, you do not need a visa to go to Mexico. There is nothing you need to do in advance of your trip. If, however, you are from one of those countries whose citizens do require a visa, you will have to visit a Mexican consulate and apply and pay for a visa that will be stamped into your passport prior to your trip to Mexico. This is much like the home-country process described earlier in this book for those applying for temporary or permanent residency, albeit with a bit less stringent requirements. Countries who fall into this latter group include a few in the Americas, such as Cuba, Brazil, Ecuador, and Nicaragua; Asian countries including China, India, Pakistan, and Philippines; and European countries such as Bosnia-Herzegovina, Serbia, Russia, Albania, and Turkey; and most countries in Africa. If you want to see a full list of countries in this category, just go to https://www.inm.gob.mx/gobmx/word/index.php/paises-requieren-visa-para-mexico/ .

It is worth noting that some folks from the countries above can essentially become visa-free types, at least for a while, if they have some sort of legal stay status in the US. For example, if a Serbian or Turk is legally in the US on an F-1 student visa, then that person may enter Mexico as a tourist without applying for a tourist visa. Another example would be those taking part in an ocean cruise. All passengers on a cruise ship are essentially free of visa requirements (assuming, of course, that they continue with the cruise when the ship leaves port).

For the no-visa-required folks, things are easy. As I just mentioned, there is nothing you need to do in advance. You just go, and when you enter the country, you will be granted a certain number of days that you can stay, up to 180 days. In the past, it was pretty much a given that you would be given 180 days upon entry, but nowadays that is not always the case. You might get 90 days or 60 days or 30 days. It is all up to the officer you run into at passport control on that day.

There are two things you should be aware of in regard to this length-of-permitted-stay topic. One is, assuming you are flying in, that you should not be given seven or fewer days because the price of your ticket includes the government fee for a greater-than-seven-days landing permit (called the FMM - and more on that in a moment). Another is that if you are granted less days than you planned on, or find yourself wanting to stay longer than you were granted permission for, there is no legal way for your to extend your stay other than to leave the country and try coming back in again. In addition, for those who are granted a 180 day stay, once you leave the country, that 180 days is over. Some people ask if they will be granted the remainder of their stay if they leave early and then come back, and the answer is *no*. There is no remainder. When you leave, that previous permission is over. You will get what they give you when you reenter, and that could be another 180 days or. . .whatever the passport control officer decides to give you.

What Is An FMM And An FMMd? How Do I Get One?

If you have not already heard of an FMM in the course of your Mexico investigations, you no doubt will at various times ahead. FMM stands for *Forma Migratoria Multiple*. Many people incorrectly refer to it as a tourist visa, but it is not that. It is a basically a traveler's permit, quite similar to the American I-94 entry and departure record (formerly card) that foreign visitors of all visa statuses (including those not requiring a visa) get while entering the US. Everyone who enters Mexico gets one, either in paper or digital form whether they are required to get a visa or not.

The FMM shows the date of entry into Mexico, the port and means of entry, and the visa or non-visa status of the entrant. Most importantly, it is where the officer at passport control jots down, usually in illegible numerals, the number of days the entrant is allowed to stay in Mexico. The FMM is free for visits of seven days or less and 680 pesos for stays of more than seven days and less than 180. That fee of 680 pesos is rolled into the price of your ticket when you fly into the country, so most visitors don't even realize that they are paying for the FMM.

In the past, the FMM was always in the form of a long card with pretty red, white, and green top and bottom borders. The flight attendants would usually distribute these on flights to Mexico just prior to the final descent into the country, and the passengers would get busy filling them out, usually happy to have something to do during the last few minutes of their flights. Once on the ground you'd hand these along with your passport to a passport control officer, who would stamp it, scrawl the number of days you are permitted in the country, and then tear off half of it along a perforated line. You would then keep the remaining half, turning it in at the departure gate when you left the country.

This has changed, however, in that the FMM has gone electronic for almost all airport ports of entry. This electronic FMM, known as an *FMMd*, is usually just a stamp placed in your passport by the passport control agent in Mexico. The agent will also scan your passport, thus recording your entry into the country electronically, after which s/he will scrawl, still usually illegibly, the number of days you are permitted to stay on the appropriate spot in the FMMd stamp. When you leave the country, your passport will be scanned again, thus recording your departure from Mexico as well. No FMM card to lose anymore.

Entering On Foot Or By Car

There is an exception to this new digital FMM experience, however, and that is when you are entering the country on foot or by car, in which case paper FMMs are still pretty much the norm, at least for now. Land borders are also slowly moving over from paper FMMs to electronic FMMds, so that is something to be aware of in the future.

At any rate, entering Mexico by land is the simplest entry process, but the FMM part of it is a bit more cumbersome. Not difficult, just a bit more cumbersome. You see at many border crossings, especially the smaller ones, things are decidedly casual, especially for pedestrian entrants. There is no gate to walk though and no officers to show passports to. There is usually nothing really except a building where some folks are doing various jobs, and almost all of them ignore you because there is nothing they are specifically supposed to do to handle you. The sole exception at some locations is the person who runs the baggage scanner, who will call you over if you come in carrying a purse or suitcase and ask you to place your bag on said scanner. That's it. Otherwise, you just walk in one door and then out the other, and. . . voilà, you are in Mexico. At bigger crossings, there might be something more of a seemingly regulated system, but the essence is the same: you walk in, you walk out, and you're there - passports often neither viewed nor touched.

Going in by car is also surprisingly easy. In this case, you drive through the American CBP side of the border (usually with no one saying anything to you), then drive into the Mexican side, and then you are guided through a gate, or one of several gates at bigger crossings, where you might just be waved through or you might be stopped and asked if you have any. . . well, whatever they are looking for that day. They might ask to see your vehicle title to make sure it is yours, and they might not. They might ask you to roll down your back windows or open your trunk or, if you are in a pickup, your truck bed. The officers will take a look, and then, assuming you're not trying to cart in something against the law. . .well, you drive out the gate and into Mexico.

OK, so when do I get my FMM if no one is checking my documents anywhere? Ah. . .well, this is where the "cumbersome" part comes into play. As I already said, at land crossings, the onus of getting your FMM falls on you. You have to get it because no one is going to tell you to, even though the law says that every non citizen entering the country must get one. When you come in by air, they are going to put you into the system, like it or not, and they are not going to let you in without doing so, so you can't avoid getting an FMM. By land, however, they let you in first, and then let you do the rest on your own volition.

There are two ways of getting your FMM for a land crossing. The first way is to get your FMM online before you go. You just go the INM's website (link below), pick your land-based destination, fill out the form, submit it online, and then if your stay is to be for 7 days or less, the FMM is free, so you will immediately be sent a link by email, from which you can download your FMM and print it out. If you plan on staying longer than 7 days, you will have to pay 697 pesos, which is about $38 US. This you can pay by card online. Once the payment is approved, you will be sent the link by email by which you can download and print your FMM.

And that's it, right? Well, no. Once you cross into Mexico, you must go the INM office there at the crossing, present your FMM and passport, and the agent there will enter your entry into the system. When you leave Mexico, go to the INM office at the border at your port of exit from Mexico (before crossing over to the US side) to record your departure. As I said, it isn't hard, but it is a tad cumbersome. The INM website for FMMs is listed below:

https://www.inm.gob.mx/fmme/publico/en/solicitud.html

The other option is to ignore the online application bit, and just go to the INM office at your point of entry, as mentioned in the description above, and fill out the FMM card in person, thus killing two birds with one stone, since you have to go to the office either way. If you have to pay the 697 peso fee because you are planning on staying longer than 7 days, there will be a Banjercito window in or next to the INM office where you can pay. Again, when you exit the country, be sure to go the INM office at your point of exit from Mexico to record your exit.

But My Friends Say They Never Bother Getting An FMM

Well, this is a claim that you will hear very often, especially online, and it is probably true. But even though it is true, that doesn't mean it is right or legal. Can you get away with it? Depends on the when and the where, I suppose. I mean look at Puerto Peñasco, Sonora, also known as Rocky Point and often jokingly referred to as "Arizona's beach." If you head down there, you and almost everyone will cross the border at Lukeville, AZ, and enter Mexico in Sonoyta, Sonora. It is a busy border, especially at holidays and on weekends, and when they have a really big event, such as the Rocky Point Motorcycle Rally, the border gets crazy and insane in terms of traffic. And yet at such times, you see almost no one stopping at the INM office to get their FMM or to get their FMM stamped.

To be honest, if people did stop to get their FMM, there wouldn't be the parking or the manpower to handle it. There would instead be so much congestion on the Mexican side of the crossing that the area would be impenetrable. Since the prosperity of everything between that border crossing and Puerto Peñasco depends on traffic through that crossing being relatively fluid, police tend not to hassle people much on that stretch, not for FMMs anyway. Go beyond that without an FMM, however, and you're fair game.

The same is true of border towns, like, for example, Mexicali, Ciudad Juárez, Laredo, Puerto Palomas, and the "dentist town" of Los Algodones. It is unlikely you'll find anyone who bothers getting an FMM to just pop into those towns, and, again, since those towns' prosperity is largely dependent on cross border customers and business, authorities do their best to not hassle visitors. Again, however, go beyond those towns into the outback, and. . . well, on your own.

So What Happens If I Get Caught Without An FMM?

Best case scenario is that you will be scolded and perhaps fined. Worst case scenario is that you will be arrested, kept in detention for a day or two, and then deported. This does happen, and it happens not only to those who do not have an FMM but those with an expired one. That all said, unless you are restricting your visit to the confines of a border town or to a well-travelled traffic corridor known to be visitor friendly or a highway where FMMs are usually obtained a few kilometers from the border rather than at the border itself (such as KM21 on the highway from Nogales to Hermosillo), get the FMM, and save yourself some potential grief. Keeping yourself legal makes you less vulnerable to corruption and abuse.

CHAPTER 7: DOING MEXICO BY CAR

Insurance, Free Zones, TIP, and More

Well, now that we've touched upon the topic of entering Mexico by car, let's talk more about the whole topic of driving in Mexico, either in a rental or in your own vehicle, either as a tourist or as a resident.

Some people are afraid to drive in Mexico, thinking it is somehow too wild a place to drive in. There are some things that are quite different and worth paying heed to, but it is not any more terrifying an experience than anywhere else in the world. Of course, perspective all depends on where you're going and what you are familiar with, and that is the same with driving in Mexico. I mean if you can drive in NYC, Mexico City should seem easy - and the traffic just as molasses like.

The Basics - Drivers Licenses And Insurance

To drive in Mexico, you need a license, just like anywhere else. The good news is that your license from back home is just fine. So whether your license is from North Carolina, Kansas, Saskatchewan, Prince Edward Island, or Bermuda, you are good to go. You are also good to go with a license from Nicaragua, Argentina, Ecuador, or any other Spanish speaking country. If, however, your license is not in English or Spanish, then you will need a so-called "international license," which is basically a translation of your license that you can get in your own country, usually from auto clubs, such as AAA or CAA, for a low cost. Remember that an "international license" is just a translation of your license, not an actual license, so it must always be presented along with your actual driver's license. Alone it means nothing.

In addition to a license, you are also legally required to carry Mexican auto insurance. Oddly, this is something people want to get cheap about. "Oh, my insurance company back home says I'm covered, so I don't need it" or "My credit card company covers me, so no need" are the kind of things you will very often hear. Well, don't listen to any of that noise. First of all, most people who give such advice have never had an accident in Mexico, and thus are only speaking from the experience of not having Mexican insurance, not from the experience of having an accident while not having Mexican insurance.

If nothing else convinces you that you need Mexican insurance, perhaps this will: if you get into an accident in Mexico, you can be put in jail until the financial matters are handled by your insurance company. The closer the insurance company is, the greater the chance they will have an agent ready to come and vouch for your coverage. Do you really want to spend a night or two in jail while you wait for your insurance company back home to find and send a rep to you in Mexico? Yeah, no. Just buy it.

Mexican insurance is not cheap, but it is not prohibitively expensive, and the longer you buy it for, the cheaper it becomes. So if you are just buying a policy for a week or two, it will seems proportionately more expensive than a six-month or year-long policy. For example, a 7 day policy for a trip to Rocky Point or to Ensenada might cost you around $150 while a six month policy would be about $375 and a full year policy $450.

Oh, and if you are towing a trailer, don't forget to insure that too!

Anyway, you can easily buy Mexican insurance online, or you can buy it from one of the shops you see along the road as you get closer and closer to Mexico. There are all sorts of insurance agents, Sanborn and Mexpro are two you will see mentioned a lot, and there are others. They are not the insurers themselves though, so your actual policy will be through companies such as El Aguila, GNP, and Chubb. At the end of the application process, you will usually get a quote which allows you to choose between policies offered by such companies, and once you make your choice, you pay, and then download and print out your policy.

From what others who have actually had to use their insurance have said, it is best to go with an agent who is local to where you will be based. Getting insurance through your American carrier doesn't really get you any perks, since what they will sell you will be through a Mexican company anyway, and getting through to an American company can be a chore that often involves a phone trip to a call center to the other side of the world. You don't want that in a crunch.

Can I Get A Mexican License?

If you are a tourist, the answer is *no*. I'm not sure why a tourist would want to waste their limited time trying to get one anyway. If, however, you are a resident, then the answer is *yes*. How you go about it depends on the state you are in since such matters are handled at the state level, just like back in the United States or Canada. In some states, you will need to take a written test, in some a written test and a driving test, and some might also require a blood test so as to accurately record and show your blood type on your license. When I got my license in Oaxaca in 2018, I didn't need much. I just needed to show my residency card and proof of address, which in my case was in the form of an electric bill furnished to me by my AirBnB owner. I asked a local friend why it was so easy to get a license, and his explanation surprised and amused me: "Well, they figure that if you don't know how to drive, you wouldn't apply for a license." Can't argue with that, I guess.

At any rate, find out what the requirements in your state in Mexico are, and then decide whether or not it is worth the trouble.

Renting A Car

Renting a car in Mexico is very common and not at all complicated. Some companies even allow one-way rentals, provided they have offices in both the pick-up and drop-off cities. You will see familiar rental company names in Mexico such as Avis, Enterprise, and Hertz, but you will another big one you'll see but might not be familiar with is Eurocar. When looking up rental costs on any of their sites, your initial reaction is sure to be "Wow! That's pretty cheap." Ah, but it is not really cheap because you also need to add the cost of their insurance, and you definitely want their insurance. The cost of the insurance is often higher than the cost of the rental itself.

If I were to offer any advice in regard to renting a car in Mexico, it would be these three things:

- Don't rent from the US via an online site, such as Expedia, etc. Things so often seem to go wrong when you do, and the car you thought you had reserved turns out not to have been, or the price you thought you had reserved the car at turns out to be a different amount entirely.

- If possible, make your reservation at an office near you rather than on the company's online site. In my experience, doing this has yielded lower rates.
- Buy the most all-inclusive insurance the company has. Don't try to save a few bucks by thinking that your insurance back home or through your credit card will do the trick. As I have mentioned elsewhere in the chapter, much trouble can follow if you go that route.

Free Zones And TIPs

Driving into Mexico is easy, but just how easy depends on where you are going, or at least how far in you're going. You see Mexico has what are known as *free zones*, also referred to as *No Hassle Zones*, where you can drive your car without any special permits. All you need, as I mentioned before, is a license, Mexican insurance, and to drive on in. The Free Zone consists of the 20 to 25km strip of land along the Mexican side of the US border; all of the Baja Penninsula; the northwestern portion of the state of Sonora, with highways 2 and 10 forming the eastern border; and at the southern border with Belize, the entire state of Quintana Roo. The idea of these Free Zones is to facilitate tourism and trade in these regions.

If you go anywhere beyond these free zones, you will need to get a Temporary Import Permit, commonly referred to as a *TIP.* TIPs are available to any tourist (FMM) or temporary resident of Mexico. As you might recall from earlier in the book, Permanent Residency holders are not allowed to drive foreign plated cars in or into Mexico. If you are a Permanent Resident and want to bring your car into Mexico, then you will need to *nationalize* it, which we will discuss at the end of the chapter.

Basically, the purpose of the TIP is to make sure you take your car back out of Mexico when you leave. In other words, they don't want you doing some sort of auto importing business. Mexico has its own auto industry to protect, after all. Well, that is what the deposit part of it is for at any rate. (Deposit? Read on.)

There are three ways you can get a TIP. The first is from the Mexican consulate near you, assuming that your consulate has a Banjercito branch. The downside to this approach is that you have to make an appointment at the consulate and then go there. As you will discover, getting an appointment at a Mexican consulate, well at some of them anyway, can be a pain. On top of that, you still have to complete the online application mentioned in the section below, so there is not much advantage in going this consulate route for your TIP.

The second way to get a TIP is do it online though Banjercito. Banjercito, in case you're wondering, is the bank of the Mexican military, and it is they who handle issuing TIPs. This involves filling out a form online, sending in scanned PDF copies of the required documents, and paying Banjercito online via credit or debit card, after which they will send you your TIP by email.

The easiest way, however (which happens to be the *only way* if you have temporary residency), is to get your TIP at the border at the Banjercito office there. The Banjercito office will be on the Mexican side of the border, just after you pass through the American side. It is usually next or close to the INM office at the border (the one where you get your FMM). On certain routes, especially routes en route to destinations popular with tourists, you can get your TIP (and FMM) at checkpoints at the end of the Free Zone. Perhaps the best known is KM21 just south of Nogales on Highway 15.

To get the TIP, you will need to present several things, all of which can be found on the Banjercito website below:

https://www.banjercito.com.mx/registroVehiculos/

The details can be a bit confusing due to the way they word things on the site and because they sort of mix the information for Mexican citizens living abroad with non-Mexican licenses with the information for foreign citizens. At any rate, here is a rundown of what they want:

1. Valid passport or passport card or green card

2. A copy of your FMM - You must get your FMM before you can get the TIP, either online or at the border.

3. A non-Mexican drivers license with photo.

4. The original title and registration for you vehicle and a copy of each. If the title or registration are in your spouse's name, then a copy of your marriage certificate is also required. If you are bringing in a company car or a rented, leased, or financed vehicle, you must provide a notarized letter of permission for the company or bank holding the lien on the vehicle.

5. Proof of temporary Mexican automobile insurance.

And that is the paperwork part of it. You also have to cough up some money too. First there is the fee for the permit itself, which is listed on the Banjercito site. Currently that amount is $911.93 MXN. Divide that by the current exchange rate to get the dollar equivalency. At the time of this writing, that comes to about $53 US. Ah, but there is more.

In addition to the fee, you also have to put down a deposit. The idea of this deposit is to get you to bring the car back home from Mexico, and thus not leave it there in Mexico and try to sell it. The amount of deposit required is tied to the age of the car:

2007 and later - $400 USD
2001-2006 - $300 USD
2000 and before - $200 USD

This is a deposit, not a fee, so when you leave the country, you will get your deposit back as long as you leave by the return date on the permit, which should mirror the date of expiry for your FMM, so, for example, if your FMM expires on September 5, your TIP will also expire on September 5. This is why you are required to get your FMM first.

Remember that it is not enough to just leave the country in order to get your deposit back. Since you also have an FMM, you already have to, or are supposed to, stop by the INM office at the border so that your exit from the country can be recorded, so going through the Banjercito exit procedures is convenient enough to do too since the INM and Banjercito are usually in the same building or same complex. Please note, however, that while you can go through INM exit procedures at any crossing you like, for the Banjercito side of things, you must exit from the same crossing you used to come into the country.

If you would like to read up more on the whole TIP process and other fine points, some of the better known Mexican auto insurance sites have excellent pages you can refer. You can access Sanborn's TIP page at https://www.sanborns.com/vehicle_permit/ , and Mexpro's TIP page at: https://www.mexpro.com/mexico/vehicle-import-permit.html

Sonora Only Permit

There is also something called a Sonora Only Permit, which covers your vehicle when driving in Sonora outside the Sonora Free Zone. Say, for example, that you drive down to San Carlos for a few weeks at the beach, but then you decide you wouldn't mind driving inland a bit to see the old colonial city of Alamos. Well, San Carlos is in the Sonora Free Zone, but Alamos, while in Sonora, is not in the Free Zone. Assuming you don't plan to drive in any other state of Mexico outside of Free Zones on this particular visit, you could buy yourself a Sonora Only TIP instead of the usual all Mexico one.

The advantage of the Sonora Only Permit is that it costs less if you pay in person in Sonora vs what you'd pay online, which is the same fee as for the regular all-Mexico TIP fee of $911.93 MXN. The other big plus of the Sonora Only Permit is that you don't have to pay a deposit. You can get the permit in person at Banjercito offices at Agua Prieta and Cananea, or if coming from the Sonora Free Zone, at the Empalme *Only Sonora* station, which is located on Highway 15 at KM 98 between Empalme and Ciudad Obregón.

Nationalization

As mentioned earlier in the book, if you have permanent residency, you cannot bring in and/or drive a foreign-plated car in Mexico. It is actually illegal. If you want to bring your car from back home you will have to go through the nationalization process, and not all cars are eligible, so if you really had your mind set on bringing your Dodge Viper V10, your Audi R8, or your Ferrarri Berlinetta in with you, sorry to smack down your dreams. There are all sorts of other restrictions too, which can make figuring it all out a bit confusing.

Luckily, in this case (since it would be a pain to figure out), nationalizing your car is not something you can do on your own. Mexico requires you to hire a customs agent *(Agente Aduanal)* to handle things for you, thus relieving you of the chore of understanding the confusing regulations.

One thing you should be aware of up front, since it might impact your decision on whether it is better to nationalize your current car or just better to buy a car in Mexico, is that nationalizing a car is expensive. For cars of the approved import age, you will be assessed a VAT of 16% of the value of the vehicle as determined by Customs. On top of that, there is an import tax that varies with the age of the car and where you are registered as living in Mexico.

That all said, it really all does add up, and many find it easier and cheaper to sell your car back home and buy a new one in Mexico, where so many models found in the US and Canada are from anyway.

Driving Tips

Driving in Mexico is not particularly complicated. Driving can be intense in some areas of some cities, but it is certainly easier than driving in Rome or Taipei. There are a few things that most expat drivers will recommend though. One of which is to not drive at night. There are many reasons for this, and just not being able to see as well is one of them. More important than that, however, is that weird things seem to happen more at night. You are more likely to find stray farm animals walking across the highway or a bed or couch that has fallen off the back of a flatbed splayed out across the road. Then there is the fact that it become hard to see *topes*, which I will discuss in greater detail in the next section. On top of all this, nefarious happenings tend to happen more often at night. That means that gang activity is more likely to happen then than during the day. That all said, avoiding driving at night is probably a very good idea.

Another thing that is often recommended is that when driving longer distances, stay on the toll roads and avoid the back roads when possible. Again, this is because you are likely to come across oddities, such as farm animals and debris from the back of trucks, but also because you will less likely fall victim to criminal activity, and, should you have a breakdown or flat tire, you can wait for assistance from the Green Angels, or *Ángeles Verdes*, who patrol Mexican toll roads and federal highways providing emergency assistance for free. You can even call them for help if you are on a toll road or federal highway by dialing 078.

Other than that, religiously obey speed limits (and remember that the posted speeds are in Km/h, not MPH), make full stops at stop (ALTO) signs (no "California Rolling Stops"), and do not make right turns on red lights. That should keep you out of the police's sights and thus out of trouble.

Topes

Ah....what nasty work these things called *topes* are. What are they? Well, they are speed bumps. But rather than the uniformly-sized and clearly-marked speed bumps back home, which are usually placed in suburban neighborhoods to keep children from getting run over by fast-moving cars, the speed bumps, or topes, in Mexico. . . are all over the place and anyplace. They can be in residential neighborhoods, on business streets, and even on toll roads! And they are not only all over the place, but they are also not at all uniform in size and not always easy to see. Drivers are usually forewarned by signs announcing their approach, but not always, so you have to really be on your guard for topes. And remember, Mexican topes are often steeper than the speed bumps you find back home, so hitting one too fast can result in damage to your car's axle, frame, or body. Some people joke that it is no coincidence that there are often body or axle repair shops located by or near topes. At any rate, topes are a part of driving life in Mexico, so *en garde*!

The Police

Americans who drive in Mexico a lot, especially those who drive from Tijuana to Ensenada and those ply the highway from Lukeville, AZ, to Puerto Peñasco, Sonora, often complain about corrupt policemen stopping them for all sorts of minor infractions or for no reason at all, suggesting that the police do this so as to get bribes, or *mordidas*.

Well, yes, this does happen, and I even experienced a case of such extortion while just being a passenger on a passenger van full of expat hikers in the middle of Oaxaca on a busy street. On that occasion, a hat was passed among us, and the driver handed the contents over to the police at the road block. As to what the driver had been accused of, I have no idea since everyone was all hush hush about it, but paying the bribe is not the recommended way of handling it.

In fact, asking for and taking a bribe is illegal. Offering a bribe is illegal too, so if you run into an honest police officer and offer him a bribe, well, you just walked yourself into an ugly hole. The recommended thing to do if asked to pay your fine there on the street to the police officer is to instead offer to go to the station and pay there. You might have to pay whatever the real fine is for whatever you are charge with, but at least you will not be contributing to corruption or compromising yourself by offering a bribe. It is a sad thing about Mexico that can really tarnish an otherwise wonderful experience.

Of course, you can't completely avoid shakedowns, but the best way to try is by avoiding getting into a situation where the problem might arise. And that means following traffic regulations to the letter. If the speed limit is 25 Km/h, drive at 25 Km/h, not 27 or 28 or whatever feels more appropriate. I mean, in the many times my wife and I have made the drive to Puerto Peñasco from Lukeville, AZ, we are continuously passed by cars with Arizona plates driving at 30 to 40 Km/h over the posted limit. Of course, we almost always get to our destination before them because just a ways down the road, we see the same cars on the side of the road getting ticketed. Karma, man.

In addition to this, people recommend having a dashcam in that it might, in theory, discourage such happenings, as no cop wants to be caught on camera engaged in such a act, but who knows. Other recommend starting up the video on your cellphone the minute you are stopped, and the policeman comes towards your car. This particular course of action is not universally well received or tolerated, and can thus land you in more trouble than when you started out. I mean, c'mon, you're not in Kansas anymore.

Will My Car Be Safe In Mexico?

This is a question that you hear a lot from people who want to drive down to Mexico but have never been there before. I guess there is the assumption by such folks that a new American car will stick out like a sore thumb down there and thus will be a target crime or vandalism. The assumption being, I guess, that most cars in Mexico will be old and in poor repair. Sorry, but not a correct assumption.

I think it safe to say that most expats are surprised when they first get to Mexico by how many new model cars there are down there. Not only are there so many new cars, there are also so many exotic (exotic to Americans, anyway) brands. I mean you never see Renaults driving around in the States anymore, but you do down in Mexico. Take a walk around the Polanco area of Mexico City, and you'll feel downright poor as you stroll past the Lamborghini, Maserati, and Mercedes-Benz dealerships. What you see all depends on where you live, but you can be pretty sure that in most urban areas, you will be surrounded by lots and lots of new, shiny cars, so don't worry too much that your car is going to stick out. Chances are, it might stick out for looking rather dowdy compared to what is around you.

If there is anything that might single you out, it could be your foreign license plate, especially to less than scrupulous policemen, so that is something you might ask around about. In general, however, it should not cause you much concern, particularly in the border states to the north, where American plates are commonly seen due to cross border traffic.

Do I Need A Car In Mexico

That all depends on where you live and what you hope to do. For many people living in the heart of the city, a car can be a hindrance. You have to park it, deal with traffic, pay for insurance, pay for gas, which is more expensive than in most states back home, and just put up with the daily hassles that driving presents. On top of that, driving insulates you from society and the life around you. You more or less miss out on half the fun and flavor of wherever you are living. Many expats who abandon driving, just use public transportation to get around, and taxis to come back from big shopping trips to the supermarket, which is a common enough practice for locals too, as evidenced by the line of taxis you will usually find waiting for fares outside most supermarkets and hypermarkets like Walmart.

For those living in smaller towns or out in the country, a car can become more of a necessity if public transportation options or taxis are less common. Some people also like to do road trips or drive off to hard-to-get-to trailheads for hiking or to out-of-the-way fishing spots and thus find having a car the best means for them to achieve what they like and want to do. And doing what you want to do or imagine yourself doing is what your move to Mexico is all about.

That said, deciding whether or not you need or want a car in Mexico is really a process of weighing pros and cons. If you are wondering whether you should bring your car, think about whether a car is necessary for what you want to do or how you want to feel in Mexico, and then, if you opt for having a car, then decide whether or not bringing your own with you is worth the hassle and costs. If you don't bring a car with you, you can always buy one down in Mexico if you find yourself wanting one.

CHAPTER 8: USING PUBLIC TRANSPORTATION

Since we were just on the topic of driving into and around Mexico, this seemed as good a spot as any to continue with the getting-around-the-country theme by switching over to the public modes of transportation offerings. After all, the majority of people who visit or move to Mexico use public transportation exclusively and have little to no interest in dealing with having a car of their own. Fortunately, it would be a pretty correct cliché to say that if there is somewhere you want to go in Mexico, there is a public transportation option there for you.

Domestic Air

Needless to say, given the very large size of Mexico, air transportation is a very useful and popular way of getting from one part of the country to the other. To give you a feeling for the distances within Mexico, the driving distance from Tijuana to Mérida is about the same as that from Los Angeles to NYC, so, well, we're talking about a big country!

Flying domestically in Mexico is pretty much like flying domestically back home, so there is not too much that needs to said about that. Just like back home, you will need some official ID in order to board a plane, and for a foreigner that is passport or, if you are resident flying domestically, your Resident Card.

It is worth mentioning by name the Mexican domestic carriers, several of which also fly internationally. AeroMexico, of course, is seen by most as the national carrier, but, in fact, it is the just recently resurrected Mexicana Airlines that is actually owned by the government.

There are also other budget airlines you might want to look into. These include Volaris, VivaAerobus, and TAR. There is also a small airline, Aerotucan, which flies small prop planes from Oaxaca City to the Oaxacan coast, notably Puerto Escondido. Airtucan can take you between these two spots in about an hour, which is about seven hours shorter than taking one of the many combis that ply the route via winding mountain roads. There is a reason such vans are nicknamed "vomit vans" by those who have given them a try. That said, if you are in a hurry or even a little prone to car sickness, look into Airtucan if you are considering making that particular trip.

Train

Mexico used to have a pretty extensive passenger rail system. In fact, my grandmother first came to the United States a few years after the Mexican Revolution through Nogales on a Southern Pacific train from Mazatlán. Now, however, there are only four rail passenger rail lines, which is actually two more than there were just a month ago, so that is progress. One train is the Tequila Express, which is essentially a tourist train that runs from Guadalajara to, you guessed it, Tequila. *Salud!*

Another is the very well known El Chepe, and there are

two versions of that train, a regular and less expensive version oriented towards local passenger traffic and which goes between the City of Chihuahua and Las Mochis, Sinaloa. The El Chepe Express is the more famous and deluxe version of the train, and is geared more towards the tourist trade, limiting its route to the Copper Canyon area, thus running only between the Pueblo Mágico of Creel, Chihuahua, and Las Mochis. There are plans to extend the route all the way into Mazatlán, so keep an eye out for that if a trip on the El Chepe is in your plans.

The third rail service is the Tren Maya, which is a new train serving the Yucatan area. The train had been talked about so long that people just assumed it would never happen, but tracks are laid, stations have been built, the trains bought, and service has begun in the segment between Campeche and Cancun, with more segments to open during the rest of the year. In addition, service has just begun on the first segment of another new train called the Trans-Isthmus Railway, or *Tren Interoceánico*, which will connect the Pacific and Gulf of Mexico at the Isthmus of Tehuantepec, near the southern end of the country.

It's worth mentioning, since you might have heard of it and wondered why I did not include it in the list above, that there was a tourist train running between Puebla and Cholula from 2019 to 2021. Unfortunately, that line was closed down due to lack of ridership, which comes as no surprise since the scheduling and frequency of trains on that line were just awful.

Intercity Highway Buses

Intercity highway buses is a public transportation segment where Mexico really shines. Riding a Mexican intercity bus is, simply put. . .really nice. Think business class on an airplane. You get lots of legroom, movies in the seatback in front of you on the luxury class buses, and clean bathrooms, usually with separate men's and women's rooms. On many lines, you are even given a snack and drink as you board. Can't beat that! Best of all the prices are quite reasonable and the number of buses per day on most routes are many.

There is no Greyhound system covering the entire country, as there is in the US, but there are several major bus companies covering certain geographic areas. For example, Autobuses Chihuahuenses serves northern Mexico from Ciudad Juárez to points as far south as Mexico City. Primera Plus is a central Mexico centered line, serving Leon, Guanajuato, Morelia, and Mexico City and Puerto Vallarta, among others locations. The more luxurious ETN, pretty much covers the same area as Primera Plus. ADO is well known to those travelling to and from Oaxaca to Puebla and Mexico City and to the western and coastal areas, including destinations such as Acapulco and Huatulco on the west coast, and cities such as Cancún, Merida, and Veracruz in the eastern central coastal area.

The level of luxury on these highway buses is excellent, but it is better on some than others. For example, ETN and Primera Plus cover many of the same destinations, but the ETN buses are much nicer. Not only do they have fewer rows of seat in the same overall cabin length (meaning much more leg room), they also have wider seats, with the Primera Plus buses have traditional 2X2 seating compared to the 2X1 seating found on ETN buses. If you are travelling alone and don't particularly want someone sitting directly next to you, this is a really great perk. Of course, the ETN buses are a bit more expensive than Primera Plus, but for a long haul, they are definitely worth the added cost.

These differences in level of luxury can also be found even within one company, and ADO is a good example. The standard ADO buses are pretty much like Primera Plus buses, nice in every way, though you won't have your own entertainment screen on the seatback in front of you. Their ADO GL buses, on the other hand, have fewer rows of seats for that added leg room. They also have two bathrooms rather than one, but ADO's highest level of first class luxury buses are the ADO Platino buses, and these are very much like the ETN buses I just described with 2X1 seating and 36 rows of seats, rather than the usual 40.

Of course, Mexico is a big country, and so there are many

other bus companies, some of which run in a large geographic area, such as the ones I've just mentioned, or those that run in a more limited regional area, such as Pullman de Morelos between Cuernavaca and Mexico City, or Albatros running between Puerto Peñasco and Guaymas, or Chapala Plus, running between Guadalajara and Ajijic and Chapala.

Almost all of these bus services have reserved seats, so you can pick whatever seat you want when you make your reservation, and thus not have to worry about any problems arising on the bus since, in my experience, people tend to respect their seat assignments, and thus those of others. In other words, you won't have to have any seat battles like there are these days on some American domestic airlines.

You can make your reservations online, at the bus station, at some travel agents, and sometimes at bus ticket kiosks placed in areas with heavy pedestrian traffic. You can also buy tickets for many lines at OXXO convenience stores, though I personally don't recommend doing that simply because the stores are often busy and the action quick, so it can be a bit hard to try to see what seats are available and to pick the ones you want, especially when doing it all in a foreign language. If the store is empty, of course, there should be no problems. At any rate, if you are going to make a reservation in person, it is still a good idea to do your research online, jot down the time of the bus you want to take and the seat/s you want on it, and then just bring that with you to wherever you are planning to make the reservation and pay for the ticket. That makes it easy for all involved and helps to ensure that you will get everything right.

It is worth noting that when trying to make reservations online, you might have problems paying with non-Mexican credit cards. Some companies' sites simply won't accept them. If so, you can try other online bus reservation services such as Reservamos (www.reservamos.mx), which usually has no problems with non-Mexican cards. Another option, assuming the bus company you're using has that option, is when it comes time to pay, select OXXO as your form of payment. You will then be sent a pick up code by email, which you then take to any OXXO store. Show them the code, pay, and within minutes you will get your tickets from the bus company by email. If those options don't work out for you, just buy your tickets in person via one of the other means just mentioned. And remember: If a company didn't accept your non-Mexican credit card online, it is possible they won't accept it in person either. Bring cash.

Subway/Metro

There are only three subway systems in Mexico, but the biggest of them is in Mexico City (the others being in Guadalajara and Monterrey). It is a really good, inexpensive, and convenient system too. Many visitors shy away from the Mexico City Metro, thinking it is dangerous, but it is no more dangerous than crowded subways anywhere in the world, and any such danger would be a fear of pickpocketing, rather than anything more nefarious than that. If you've ridden the subways in big American cities, then you will feel more than at home in the Mexico City Metro. If you don't have any subway riding experience, you will soon get the hang of it. Lines are clearly marked and color coded, and there is only one price for the whole system, which is still 5 pesos per ride. So whether you are going just one station or making two connected line transfers all the way to the opposite side of town, the fare will be 5 pesos. Can't beat that!

There are four things that you might find surprising about the system, though, so I will mention them here. First, the cars are not air conditioned, so it can get a bit stuffy on hot days, especially at rush hours. Second, the length of time the doors are open for boarding and unboarding is pretty short, so be prepared to move quickly. A third thing is that there is often a women-only car on most lines, and those women-only cars have roped-off and thus clearly defined women-only boarding zones within the subway station. Of course, women can and do ride in any car they like, but if you are a woman and feel safer in a women-only car, they are there for you.

Finally, you will surely be surprised to see vendors getting on the train and suddenly, once the doors close, starting their sales spiel for all to hear. They then make their way through the subway car to allow passengers to buy whatever it is they are selling (headphones were a popular item last time I was there), but don't worry, the vendors don't push. People who want whatever they're selling, give the vendor a nod, and the vendor comes their way to make the sale. When the doors open at the next station, the vendor hops off and heads to the next car. It is actually sort of interesting.

Local Buses

Local buses vary greatly from city to city. In some cities, like Mexico City, they can be quite modern and new, while in others, such as Guanajuato and Oaxaca, they are old and in bad need of shocks. Either way, they get you where you want to go and are a great way to get around town for a reasonable price. On top of that, you get a feeling of being a part of the city, a feeling you miss out on if you only travel around in the isolated cocoon of a taxi or Uber.

While getting around the country is pretty straightforward on highway buses, getting around on city buses can be a bit confusing, again depending on the city. In some cities, figuring out what the lines were and where they go is not always an easy chore. You can't just go online and find a site that tells you which bus or buses to take if you want to go from point A to point B. No, to figure out how to do that, you often have to ask around. Usually someone at your hotel or AirBnB, or your landlord, can tell you that sort of thing, so not to worry.

In some cities, especially those with the older buses for some reason, you might experience a vendor, like on the subway in Mexico City, but you might also experience a magician, or a singer, or guitarist, or a singer and guitarist getting on the bus and doing their thing and then passing the hat. Again, you are not obliged to give anything if you are not so inclined, and many do not, but then again many do. Some of the performers are quite a fun experience and break up the monotony of the bus ride.

Bus fares vary city by city, and in big cities like Mexico City, by type of bus as well. In most cities, however, fares are quite reasonable, usually in the 8 to 15 peso range. One thing you will find on the older buses in some cities is that the drivers make change, something that hasn't been happened on buses in the States for decades! It's almost worth it not to have exact fare so as to experience that little bit of nostalgia.

Taxis And Ubers

A lot of people have a great fear of taxis in Mexico, and there is some justification for this, especially in view of the past, when some unscrupulous drivers would drive out of towners to the middle of nowhere and rob them or worse. . or drop them off with ne'er-do-wells who would do the same. Of course, that was not all taxis and not everywhere, and it certainly is not the case anymore.

Airports and major bus stations now have taxi counters in the lobby where you tell the clerk where you want to go, and then s/he looks at what fare zone the destination is in, and basically sells you a ticket for a taxi. You then go outside and get in the waiting line for the taxis (these are quite quick moving, so fear not), get in the taxi that pulls up when your turn comes, hand the ticket to the driver, and off you go. No money passes hands between you and the driver, and no question of what the fare is going to be since you've already paid. If you want to give a tip to the driver at the end of the ride, you can do that, of course. All very safe and easy.

Taxis within the city. . .well, that all depends what city you are in. Just remember that taxis are generally not metered, so make sure you agree on the fare before you get in the cab. Most cities have one or two regular cab networks, so if you want to play it safe, find out what they are and stick to them. You can also ask the concierge at a hotel to call a taxi for you if that makes you feel better.

Some people prefer to take Uber, and Uber exists in Mexico. . .in some locations. Mexico City and Puebla are big Uber markets, while some other cities, like Oaxaca or Tlaxcala, have no Uber service at all due to significant, and often slightly violent opposition by the taxi drivers. Also, even in some areas that do have Uber service, there might be some destinations that are off limits or that allow drop offs but not pickups. These are things to check into wherever it is you happen to be travelling to or around.

One thing to consider when it comes to Uber is that sometimes the cars can be quite small, so if you are travelling in a group or with a lot of baggage, you might want to make sure you can be accommodated. If you are wondering how Uber works in Mexico, it is all the same as back home. In fact, you even use the same app, so all should be smooth sailing for you in that regard.

Colectivos

I remember reading a post on FB once by a couple of tourists who had just visited the big mercado in Oaxaca, Central de Abastos. It ended by their shocked recollection of taking a taxi to leave, and then being aghast when the driver picked up a few more fares. They first felt afraid and then cheated by what had transpired, and per their misunderstanding of events, they were fully right to feel so. However, one detail in their report that made it clear that what had happened was a misunderstanding. They mentioned that they had gotten into a "red taxi." In Oaxaca, red taxis are not taxis in the traditional sense, though there are conventional taxis all over the city, but rather these red colored taxis are something different. They are what is known as *colectivos*.

Colectivos are something of a cross between taxis and buses.

They are like taxis in form in that they are usually sedans, and, for some reason or another, they are very often older Nissan Sentra sedans (older models called Tsuru in Mexico). They are also like taxis in that you can flag them down while they are driving down the road. On the other hand, they are like buses in that they most often travel along set routes with the final destination shown on a card in the front window. If your destination is not on the route, you will either need to take a different colectivo or get off at some known point where you can transfer to a different colectivo route that will take you where you want to go. Of course, you can get on or off a colectivo anywhere along its route, though there is usually some sort of set pickup and dropoff spot at each end of the route. Colectivos are also like buses in that they take more than one fare. In fact, they will take as many fares as can fit in the car. Usually this would suggest 4 passengers, 3 in back and 1 up front next to the driver, but I've been in colectivos with two in the front seat, and 5 in the back seat, so laps of strangers are indeed sometimes used for extended seating.

This might sound a bit bizarre to you, but after you've taken one colectivo ride, it will feel sort of fun. More importantly, the ride will be very cheap, which is the main draw of colectivos. How much a ride is will vary depending on the city, route and how far you are going, but the fare will be far less than that for a taxi, and less than that for a bus.

Combis

Combis are essentially the same thing as colectivos but in microbus rather than sedan form. Some cities have well organized combi systems in lieu of an actual bus system, as is the case in Tlaxcala city, and/or used them as medium distance buses. Basically the same rules of ridership that apply to colectivos also apply to combis.

Combi seating is usually more comfortable than colectivo seating because there is more room. . .well, knee room at any rate, but it depends on the seating layout of the combi you are in. In some combis, the seats are arranged around the perimeter of the combi, so that everyone is essentially sitting in an inward facing circle (well, ok, a rectangle), while on others, there will be four rows of seats facing front, with acess to the right side of each row.

There is one thing to beware of when it comes to this latter type of arrangement, however, and that is that the aisle might not stay an aisle for long if things get crowded. Many, if not most, of this sort of combi have fold-down aisle seats. This means that you might think you will have some space to the right of you when you get on, only to find a seat and another passenger suddenly appearing and cramming you securely into place.

Mototaxis

Mototaxis are, as you might imagine, motorcycle driven taxis. Basically a mototaxi an extended motor trike (1 wheel up front, 2 in back), with a 3-person passenger seat, all with a roof on top. You will not find these throughout the country, but you will find them in certain parts of certain cities, usually on the outskirts, where they provide short-distance service from main roads to destinations a mile or two away. In that capacity, they usually operate like colectivos, picking up more than one fare if space permits. In rural areas, they might actually function as the sole form of local public transportation.

Camionetas

In some locations, usually very rural ones, you might come across what are often called *camionetas*, though they may go by different names in different locations. Camioneta means pickup truck, and that is essentially what camionetas are - pickup trucks that have been modified to accommodate passengers. The accommodations consist of bench seats running along the sides of the truckbed for passengers to sit on, and some sort of frame over the bed, so as to provide something for standing passengers to hang onto. This also serves as structure over which to place a tarp or over covering during times of bad weather. There is also usually a step or two at the very back to facilitate boarding.

You will usually find camionetas. . .well, off in the boonies. If you want to go, for example, by public transportation from the famous, and lovely, archeological site and Pueblo Mágico of Mitla to the very famous (and, in my opinion, highly overrated) Hierve de Agua, both just south of Oaxaca, your means of transportation will be camioneta.

CHAPTER 9: SEE MEXICO FIRST

Now that you know how to get around Mexico, it is time to get down to the topic of actually visiting it. That chapter title might sound a bit like one of those slogans from state tourist bureaus in the US promoting local tourism, but, as you might have guessed, I am not suggesting you see Mexico before some other country, or even before your own. No, I am saying that you should visit Mexico before deciding to move there. That might sound like a no brainer, but a lot of people do just that, or rather the opposite. They move down to Mexico, sight unseen, and assume all will work out as they had imagined or heard, meeting with, of course, varying degrees of success or failure.

There are a number of reasons why you should go and do some exploring and experiencing in Mexico before deciding to move there. First of all, you can see how you feel about the place and whether or not you are going to feel comfortable and at home there. Secondly, you can see where you might want to move to. Even if you've been to some place in Mexico before and think you'd like to live there, going there specifically with the mind to see what it would be like to live there is really a different thing from visiting as a tourist.

I remember visiting Oaxaca for the first time as a tourist and thinking it was really great. I couldn't wait to go back and have more *memelitas* and hot chocolate, Oaxaca style tamales, and *tlayudas*. Ah, and then at night sampling mezcals at one of the several mezcal bars in town. Seemed like a wonderful plan. And yet, when I went down again later to check it out as a place to live, I was not as enamoured. All those features I had imagined before, I quickly tired of, and the realities of day to day life there forever and ever, seemed like a prison sentence. That said, you owe it to yourself to have a look at a place through the eyes of a potential resident before you choose it as a forever home.

Visiting Through The Eyes Of A Potential Resident

So, how does one look at a place through the eyes of a potential resident? Well, for some folks that will come naturally enough, but basically it means to go to a place and approach it as if you lived there. First of all, stay in an AirBnB apartment, not a room or hostel or hotel. Something small is fine, but you want to have a kitchen and some sort of separate living space. I mean a living room and bedroom would be nice, but even a single apartment type setup would be fine at first. With that, you won't have to limit your culinary experiences to restaurants or food stands and you won't feel cooped up as you might in a hotel room.

Instead you can, and should, go to the markets, the mercados, whatever there is in town, and buy some groceries. Don't get a haircut before the trip, get your hair done down there. Develop a walking routine to get from your apartment to the store or to the ice cream stand or to the park. If you live in one of the many cities that offer free concert performances, go listen to some classical music. If you see a green market at the park, buy a plant, even if you are only going to be there for a week or two. The whole idea is to do things you would do if you actually lived there. Sure, you can take in a museum or two, but don't make seeing all the sites in town your goal on this sort of trip. Take in a few, as you might do in the ordinary course of your day as a resident, and then fill the rest of your day with normal every day activities as you do back home.

One thing I strongly recommend, regardless of your level, is to study Spanish at a language school in Mexico. I recommend this so strongly that I have dedicated the next chapter to the topic. Why? Well, not only will learning and practicing some Spanish help you in your future Mexico endeavors, but going to a language school will help you develop a routine, a routine that helps to give you a feeling of being a resident rather than a tourist. Ah, but more on that in the next chapter. . .

Where To Go

You might already have some places in mind to visit as a potential future resident, but many of you won't. To you falling into this latter group, and if you are not committed to a beachside destination, I would offer, as a first suggestion, Guanajuato.

Guanajuato is a lovely colonial city that gives one the feeling of walking through a postcard. Some friends who visited called it "instant Mexico," due to its traditional feel and very colorful look. In fact, it is said that the Disney animated film Coco was inspired visually by Guanajuato.

On top of its visual attributes, Guanajuato also has a lot of Spanish language schools, and as it is a university town whose university has a linguistics school, there are also a lot of language teachers. Best of all, it is only a 60 to 90 minute bus ride to San Miguel de Allende, Dolores Hidalgo, and Querétaro, meaning that you can take a day trip or two during your time there so as to see if one of those other locations might interest you. Oh, and if you are a bit more adventurous, the city of Morelia in Michoacan, which attracts some expats, is only a 4 hour bus trip away.

Another spot that might be of interest is the city of **Puebla**. Puebla is a big, beautiful and historic city. . . with very good food. It is also the birthplace of the day celebrated around the world, *Cinco de Mayo,* which is *not,* as many seem to believe, Mexican Independence Day. Rather, it is the day that the Mexicans defeated the French in the Battle of Puebla in 1862. In fact, Puebla is just about the only place in Mexico where the day is celebrated, which is why Mexicans from the rest of the country are always a bit surprised when they find non-Mexicans abroad celebrating it, particularly with such jubilant (i.e., drunken) fervor.

On top of that claim to fame, Puebla is also the home of Talavera pottery, and there are thus several Talavera workshops in the city, the most famous of which is probably Uriarte Talavera, which not only sells beautiful pieces, but is also a lovely place in its own right, and thus worth a visit, even if you are only mildly interested in pottery. Finally, Puelba is home to several well-respected language schools, and it is also close to other small cities that might be of interest to you to check out as potential places to live, such as Cholula, Tlaxcala, and Atlixco. It is also only a two-hour bus ride to Mexico City. In fact, a very convenient perk to visiting Puebla is that if you fly into CDMX, you can take an Estrella Roja bus directly from the Terminal at CDMX to downtown Puebla!

Finally, there is the City of **Oaxaca** in the southern part of the country. Oaxaca is a very popular colonial city with both foreign and Mexican tourists due to its very visible and influential indigenous population (mostly Zapotec) and culture, and because of its cuisine, which rivals that of Puebla in terms of popularity. It is also home to several well-regarded Spanish language schools, and is quite well renowned for its *Dia de los Muertos* festivities, during which time it is very crowded. It is also worth noting that Oaxaca also has a lot of resident expats and thus there are quite a few amenities there for and usually organized by them, particularly through the Oaxaca Lending Library, which is, incidentally, where I first met my wife at one of their Monday morning Intro to Oaxaca info sessions!

The Oaxaca Lending Library, or OLL, not only is a library with a fairly big collection of books in English, it is also a hangout of sorts, where expats can sit and have a cup of coffee or a snack, play a game of dominoes, mahjong, or bridge, and sit and shoot the breeze with whomever is there at the time. The OLL also conducts hikes and outings for a reasonable fee every month. If you are planning on visiting Oaxaca, it is definitely worth checking them out beforehand so as to see what they have planned during your stay.

Exploring For Exploration Sake

Some of you, of course, might not have yet committed to living in Mexico, or only have moving to Mexico as a notion in your mind but not a sure thing. For such folks, you might first want to just see as many places as you can during any trip you take. In a-two week period, I think you can comfortably and somewhat meaningfully get an idea of three of four places within a general region. The options are endless, but I will mention a few so as to give you some ideas that might serve as models for itineraries of your own.

In the previous section of this chapter, I mentioned some itineraries based on locations with a focus on getting a feel for living in the place. Well, all of those itineraries work well even for hubs of exploration as well if you don't care about living in Mexico or studying Spanish, since the anchor sites in each of them is worthy of checking out touristically on its own.

In addition to those I already mentioned, let me also throw in a couple of other possibilities for purposes of touristic exploration. Let me first start with Guadalajara, Mexico's second largest city. Guadalajara is quite popular with tourists because of its fame, due to its size, and its artisanal market towns, particularly Tlaquepaque and Tonalá. It also attracts a lot of tourists who want to visit the town of Tequila (for obvious reasons), or who want to have a look at the Lake Chapala towns Ajijic and Chapala. Some also use it as a launching pad to visit the city of Tepic in Nayarit, or the beach city of San Blas in the same state. Speaking of the beach, Puerto Vallarta is only a six-hour bus ride away, while back inland, the Pueblo Mágicos of Nochistlán and Teúl de Gonzáles Garcia, both in the neighboring state of Zacatecas, are also only a 2 to 3 hour bus ride away.

Finally there is CDMX - Mexico City! Many people want to avoid Mexico City because they somehow think that it is un-Mexican. That is very odd thinking because Mexico City is probably one of the most Mexican places you can think of going. It is a city with a true pulse and so many beautiful and historic places that it is said that when a man is tired of Mexico City he is tired of life. Well, OK, so they didn't say that about Mexico City. In fact, Samuel Johnson said that about London, but I would argue that is was only because he had never been to Mexico City!

Mexico City is so chock full of places to see and things to do that you could fill up two weeks just exploring the city itself. Not only does it have an amazing collection of museums, including the world class National Museum of Anthropology; but also the fun and quirky Antique Toy Museum, the Frida Kahlo Musem, located at what was her home and studio in Coyoacán, Casa Azul); and the nearby Leon Trotsky Museum, located at his former home. If you are film buff and fan of the Mexican film director, Emilio "El Indio" Fernandez Romo, you can even take a tour of his amazing home.

Of course, Mexico City is at the heart of the nation, and thus it makes a great starting off point to many other parts of the country, many of which are easily accesible by highway bus. Puebla is only 2 hours away, lovely Tlaxcala only 2.5 hours away, Cuernavaca is only 1 hour away, and Xalapa, Veracruz, which is only about 30 minutes away from the Pueblo Mágicos of Coatepec and Xico, is only a five hour bus trip away.

CHAPTER 10: STUDYING SPANISH

I suppose it sort of goes without saying that studying Spanish for those planning to live in or just visit Mexico is a good idea. Can you get by in Mexico without learning Spanish? Depending on where you are, probably, but do you really want to do that, or I suppose I should say *not* do that? Whatever level of proficiency you reach in Spanish, even if it is very low, you will get a lot more mileage out of your Mexico experience if you at least give studying Spanish a go. It doesn't matter if you are lousy at languages or have a brain like a sieve so that everything in soons drains out, you will still get something out of the process even it doesn't seem like it to you at the time.

Study Before You Go

It is always a good idea to start studying in advance of your first visit, and as I said earlier in the book, I think studying in Mexico during that first visit is a wise thing.

To get started, the free app Duolingo is a fun way to go. It gets you used to and familiar with Spanish vocabulary, and you might also start being able to deduce a bit of grammar in the process. It is also a great idea to buy a textbook and work through that on your own. Unfortunately, too many books are geared to class learning and are thus hard to use on your own. Personally, in my language learning experience, the best book for self learning that I've found is an oldie but goodie: *Madrigal's Magic Key to Spanish: A Creative and Proven Approach.* You can find it on Amazon and at bookstores in Mexico, and it is rather inexpensive. It is sort of dull looking inside, but it is easy to use. . .and it has "illustrations by Andy Warhol," which seems an odd thing to find in a book of its nature, but, hey, *¡Es lo que es!* Oh, and as an FYI, it also just so happens to be the same book my wife started her Spanish studies with.

Of course, all of this self-study is a good start, but it is all primarily reading comprehension oriented, which is nothing to sneeze at. If, however, you want to feel as if you are making some real headway, it will give you great confidence to be able to say what you want to say in Spanish, at least to some degree, and to do that, you need someone on the other end. That is why working with a teacher down the line is a good next step.

One way to get working with a teacher is to take classes at the local community college or community center, but it will not be a one-on-one setup there. You will be in a class, and you will find that very often 99% of the speaking done in class is in English, and that is just the teacher. As a student, you might very well have very very little opportunity to speak, so that might not be the ideal approach to take, though your local situation might vary. Another way, and a very good way at that, is to take an online private lesson once or twice a week with a teacher in Mexico, either via a language school there or one that is recommended to you.

Working with a teacher online one on one gives you 100%

of the class time. You can work out with the teacher what you would like to cover, and you can tell your teacher how much or how little English you would like him or her to speak. You can zero in on what you would like to do or follow along with what they have for you if you don't have a preference of your own. You are the customer, and so you have the final say.

You can take such online lessons via a Spanish language school in Mexico or with a known Spanish language tutor/teacher that you find in a Facebook group or via personal recommendation. Ideally, if you know where you are going to go on your first trip to Mexico, it might serve you well to pick a teacher from that location so that you can get some inside advice about the town and even continue lessons there with that school or teacher. I should add that if you are planning to go visit and live in Mexico, then pick a teacher from Mexico, not from Spain or Central or South America. You want to know what x is in Mexico, not in Nicaragua.

Study While In Mexico

When you finally head down to Mexico for your initial explorations, studying during your time there is, as I mentioned before, the best way to follow up your online studies. In addition to giving you more Spanish practice, you will also get a rhythm of life that might give you more of a feeling of it would be like living there, rather than that feeling of just passing through where time becomes just a random blob you flail around in. Hmm. Well, you catch my drift.

As to where to do this *study-cation*, probably, the most popular destinations for Spanish language study in Mexico are Guanajuato and Oaxaca, with Puebla having fewer yet quite famous programs of it s own. And of course, there are schools in other cities as well, such as San Miguel de Allende, Guadalajara, and Mexico City.

To give a bit of opinion to those not sure where they want to go, to my mind, Guanajuato is a great place to start. Not only is it probably one of the prettiest cities in the country, it has so many language schools that you will have plenty of choices. The fact that Guanajuato is a university town with a university that has a linguistics department means that there are lots of teachers to fill the the staffs of those schools and lots of private teachers as well. And as I mentioned before, it is also convenient to San Miguel de Allende and many other popular destinations, so lots of day trips by bus are an easy possibility.

Frustrations

No matter what language one studies, frustrations are bound to come about in your language acquisition journey. Sometimes it is the feeling one is not where one had expected to be at a certain point in time, or the feeling that one is getting worse rather than better, or that certain grammar points are just beyond comprehension (the subjunctive seems to be one such point for many folks). Well, that is all the normal course of things in language learning.

In my own case, my frustration came when my hearing started getting worse. Before moving to Mexico, during my visits and in my online classes, I was doing pretty OK, and my progress seemed steady. However, when I finally moved down, age was catching up with my ears, and suddenly I was comprehending less and less. Classrooms seemed to be more like echo chambers, and, well, things just seemed to all be going haywire - as if I was listening to the world through a paper cup. I thus lost confidence in production as well. I could barely get my simplest thoughts across, and I started feeling rather sour and acting a bit cranky.

Fortunately, it was a phase. A bump in the road, so to speak. No, my hearing did not get better, but once I realized what was happening, I was able to deal and not beat myself up about it. And that is how it is for all learners. Hurdles come in different forms, and as long as one does not give up, one gets over those hurdles, or learns to ignore them, and things level out again. OK.

Well, end of pep talk.

One other kind of frustration that you might experience, and it is one of the great ironies of language learning, especially for native English speakers, that when you go out all bound and determined to speak Spanish, Spanish speakers who are fluent or capable enough in English seem to come out of the woodwork. And it is some sort of weird universal truth too. It is not just Spanish speakers. No matter where you are in the world, an English speaker's trying to speak the native language gets the natives to search deep within and start speaking English, even though they didn't seem to know any when you tried to speak to them in English. If you are really gung ho on learning, that can be frustrating. If you are happy to just get by in English, well, studying Spanish can ironically help you in that way too.

So what does one do when this linguistic impasse comes about? Well, if I learned one thing from my wife, it is to stick to your guns and keep speaking Spanish, even if the other interlocutor fails to follow suit. I had tended to just give up and get sort of cranky in my heart of hearts at such moments, but she seems to just not even notice and keeps on ordering or whatever it is in Spanish, and at the end, all things are fine and dandy. So, don't give up, but don't be mean about it, if you know what I mean.

Language Exchange

If there is ever one form of learning I do not recommend, it is language exchange, at least not for the purpose of language learning and practice. Yeah, it sounds like a great deal, but it almost never is. Almost always there is more English being spoken than Spanish (or whatever the other language is), and even though you think you are participating in a great mutual back-scratching endeavor, somehow the Spanish speaker ends up speaking almost entirely in English, especially since the English speaker very often ends up using English as a crutch, and thus ends up not really using his or her mind to think in

Spanish, opting instead to revert to English at the first sign of uncertainty of expressing.

Sure, language exchange is fine if it is just done for having something to do on a Saturday morning or as a means of doing a sort of public service, but it is not a very useful way of learning Spanish. One of the two people is invariably dissatisfied, at least in terms of the language learning side of things.

Payment

Prices of classes at language schools, private lessons, and online lessons can vary greatly, and a higher price does not always reflect a better experience. In fact, my wife and I had a private teacher when we were in Oaxaca, and he was quite good and not at all unreasonable in terms of price, but he had a strange way of thinking, at least to my mind, when it game to his overseas online rates. He charged overseas online students almost twice as much as he did local students meeting face to face, which seemed odd since doing a face-to-face class involves time and effort getting from place to place, while online classes can be taught from home. I asked him why he did that, and he said, quite matter of factly, "because they can afford more because they are abroad." To me that sounded somehow outrageous, but there are some expats who think it is perfectly just and fair. And so, it seems, gentrification is born. . .

As for the mode of payment, most online schools or private teachers these days prefer payment via PayPal, while those you deal with in person in Mexico usually take and prefer cash, thus making everything quite easy.

Coca-Cola
HOTDOGS
CHON
HOTDOGS

CHAPTER 11: WHERE TO LIVE

Part of your planning and/or pre-visa research missions to Mexico, as well as your first weeks or months in Mexico, will be focused on finding a place to live. I'm not talking about looking for an apartment or house, at least not in this chapter, but rather a city and neighborhood therein. The problem is that Mexico is a big country with a great deal of geographic, climatic, and cultural diversity. There are plenty of popular spots along the coasts, but most cities are located in the central plateau at altitudes from 4000 to nearly 8000 feet. Mexico City, for example, seemingly flat city that it is, is situated at 7380 feet, putting it way above the "Mile High City" of Denver, which stands at a mere 5830 feet.

Many other central plateau cities popular with large expat populations also fall at elevations higher than Denver. These cites of the central plateau have generally dry mild climates, while cities along the coast, being both located in lower altitudes and at tropical or subtropical latitudes, are essentially hot and humid with the exception, I suppose, of Baja California from the Ensenada area to the US border. In other words, latitude and elevation matter.

On top of climate, people are also looking for certain characteristics: cultural amenities, a large expat community or few to no expats, lower cost of living, good food, safety, nearby airport, and so on. Often the list of desirables is also a list of contradictions. A cool summer beach town is not something you are going to find. An expat-rich community with low cost of living is, again, pretty much a contradiction, as where you have a lot of expats, you tend to have higher prices. That all said, figuring out where to live is hard when it comes to stats and checklists, but with a little groundwork and a real and honest self-evaluation of what you want and need, it actually gets easier.

Living Where The Expats Live - Pros And Cons

Since you are planning on being an expat, one of the things you must decide is whether or not you want to live in the midst of other expats or as far detached from them as possible. That seems to be one of the main choices people start off their search with. In some ways, it seems a silly point to obsess over since there are other more important things to consider. Nevertheless, the presence or dearth of expats in a potential living place is something that many people start off with a stated preference for, and there are reasons for these two points of views, some of which are quite logical and valid reasons, while others seem mere forms of prejudice rather than reflections of reality.

One of the oft touted pros of an area with a fair share of expats is that living in such a place can make it much easier for you to start out your life in Mexico. Language is less of a barrier since in such areas many businesses are often English friendly, with bilingual staff, menus, signage, etc. More importantly, there will be lots of other expats there who are or have recently been in the same boat as you: new, and somewhat lost, in a new country and just trying to make a go of it. Such people often have tips for you on how to do this or that, or they might know the perfect person to help you realize what it is you want to do - a realtor, a handyman, a cook, etc. If you are a church going type, expat areas most often have one or two churches with services in English as well. And when it comes to learning Spanish, many, though not all, expat-rich areas tend to have schools and/or private tutors for learning Spanish. As I already pointed out elsewhere, cities with good sized expat populations also often have community centers or expat-oriented or expat-run libraries that organize activities a newcomer might like to participate in.

On the down side, the expat communities themselves are smaller and more insular communities than the immediate world around them. If your happiness is gained by membership in such a community, remember that it can be taken away by the same - sort of like membership in a clique in high school.

If part of the reason for leaving home was getting away from certain types and to be with people more like yourself, well, you are likely not going to gain any ground in Mexico since the same dichotomy exists in the expat communities there. In fact, the communities being smaller and often tighter, you may find yourself more annoyed with your fellow expats than you were back home. That is life, so be prepared, or rather don't expect anything different in that department.

Finally, if you want to get into learning Spanish right away and improve as quickly as possible, then being around a bunch of people who speak the same language as you is not going to do much other than to help you maintain your English language skills. Expat areas are not ideal for L2 acquisition.

If you are considering moving to an expat area, be prepared for some people being very critical of your choice. Many expats, you see, are down on expats moving to expat areas. They tend to label such expat-rich communities as *gringolandias* and make such spots out as if they are void of Mexicans. That assertion is, of course, patently absurd. I mean the expat population of San Miguel de Allende, perhaps the most famous of expat enclaves, and one often described as the epitome of gringolandia, is only 6.25% of the total population. Just for comparison, Asians make up 15% of the population of Seattle, and yet no one calls or thinks of Seattle as an Asian city. So, you see, it is all a matter of perspective and attitude.

So what are these jammed-to-the-gills expat centers? Well, of course, we just mentioned the most famous of them all, San Miguel de Allende. Despite what the naysayers have to say, it does have a lot going for it, which is why it is also extremely popular with Mexican tourists as a weekend tourist destination and even for well-heeled folks from Mexico City wishing to buy a weekend getaway.

The second most famous is Ajijic and the Lake Chapala area. While not as famous to the outside tourist world as San Miguel de Allende, Ajijic is very popular with expat retirees, and it has the highest percentage of expat population of any place in Mexico. Expats like it for the slow pace of life, close proximity to the big city and airport (Guadalajara), its quaint cobblestone streets, and its lakeside location, though the lake is polluted and thus not good for swimming or fishing, making it more of a decorative asset.

As to what comes third, it's hard to say, but one contender is definitely the City of Oaxaca, which, as I mentioned earlier in the book, is a popular destination for both expats and Mexicans alike due to its less polished colonial charm, its rich indigenous culture, its food scene, and...mezcal. Another contender would be Puerto Vallarta, right there on seaside in the western part of the State of Jalisco. It is a true beach town, well, city, with all the amenities that go with it. . .and, unfortunately, the humidity as well. On the opposite side of the country in the State of Yucatan is another contender - Mérida. Mérida is well liked by expats because it is a laidback colonial city that is relatively inexpensive. And while not on the beach like Puerto Vallarta,

Mérida is pretty close, with its closest beach being in Progresso, about 30 miles away. One thing about Mérida that all will agree on is that it is. . . hot, and at that latitude and low elevation, humid!

Cuernavaca is another place that has a lot of expats. In fact, it used to be THE expat destination in Mexico, for not only retirees but also for students and celebrities. These days, however, the city doesn't attract as many expats as it once did, so the ones that are there are older than the average retires, and, it seems, better heeled as well. Cuernavaca is also popular with tourists from Mexico City, which is only an hour bus ride away, largely due to what is seen as its better climate. It is, in fact, nicknamed "the city of eternal spring," though in our own five-month experience there, it felt more like the city of eternal summer. I suppose climate change has taken its toll on Cuernavaca.

Of course, there are many others. Ensenada, Tijuana, Mazatlán, Tulum, Querétaro, Guanajuato, Guadalajara, and even Puerto Peñasco (Rocky Point) are also places that attract expats. And let's not forget Mexico City. Lots of expats live there, as it is a big, international, world-class city. Given its size, however, you don't really notice the expats there much.

Climate

While the expat question is on the minds of many when asking for advice on where to live, climate is probably the second most specified concern. Figuring out the climate of a particular area is not that difficult as it all more or less follows a basic pattern. As I mentioned earlier, if you want to live near the beach, count on humidity and high temperatures, with the exception of upper Baja. If you want to avoid cold winters, at least very cold winters, avoid those places at very high elevations, such as Zacatecas, Puebla, Tlaxcala, Toluca, and pretty much the entire State of Chihuahua. If you want mild summers, then you probably can't do better than some of the places I just mentioned, particularly Zacatecas, Puebla, and Tlaxcala. Another city popular with cool-summer-loving expats is San Cristóbal de las Casas in the southern state of Chiapas. Some, however, find it just too wet to deal with most of the year.

For many expats and Mexicans alike, the Central highlands of Mexico, also known as the Bajio, has the best overall climate. This area includes the cities of Guanajuato, San Miguel de Allende, Querétaro, Leon, Dolores Hidalgo, and Aguascalientes. Although not part of the Bajio, Morelia and Mexico City are considered to have a relatively similar climate. Here you can look for warm and dry summers and somewhat cold winters with no snow. If I hadn't known that it doesn't snow in the area before, I could have guessed it when I was there in Guanajuato because during that short time they experienced their first snow in over twenty years, and its people went a bit giddy. Newspapers announced the freak storm with big headlines and photos of buses that had slipped off the highway. Of course, by 11AM, when the sun came out, you would never have known that it had snowed just that very morning. Freak snowstorms aside, the weather there is pretty nice. The sun is strong, so beware the "mad dogs and Englishman" thing, and you'll be fine.

At any rate, when searching rainfall, humidity, and temperatures for any given place (in the world), an excellent resource is Weatherspark (www.weatherspark.com). There you will find all the information on almost every major, and many a minor, city throughout Mexico. Compare the results for wherever you're considering to that of some place back home that you know using the site's compare function, and you can get a pretty good idea of what a place is like.

What Do Your Like To Do?

I suppose this section can be filed in the stating-the-obvious category, but when choosing a place to live or places to check out, look for places compatible with your interests or desires. If, for example, you love going to classical concerts or visiting museums, it would make little sense to consider Puerto Peñasco,

Sonora, which is basically a beach town geared to, it would seem, giving Arizonans a place to enjoy the sand and surf. With only one museum, a small gallery at that, it is not exactly going to meet your needs. If, on the other hand, hanging out at the beach or slugging down a lot of cold ones every night is your primary concern, then Puerto Peñasco could be what you're looking for, especially if you like seafood. Conversely, cities like Mexico City, Puebla, and Oaxaca are rich in cultural amenities and are famous for their food scenes and cuisines.

My Own Suggestions

If someone were to ask me where they should check out to live without any other parameters by which to limit my suggestions, I would come up with the following locations, all highly influenced by my own personal preferences and tempered by my own experiences. That said, take the suggestions with a grain of appropriately seasoned salt. Most of these places I have already mentioned as spots to visit, so I won't be going into much personal detail on those here. I just want to offer them up for you to consider and research.

Guanajuato

As I mentioned earlier, Guanajuato is a beautiful city with a pretty great climate. It is conveniently located to other cities, and it is small enough to walk easily, and and there are lots of lovely *plazuelas* where you can sit to take a rest and watch the world go by. The food is pretty good, especially the street food options, and there is a free civic concert hall, some museums, and, as I also mentioned before, there are lots of Spanish language schools.

On the downside, it is a very hilly city, which can be tiresome if you are living there and have to carry home 20 lbs of kitty litter, especially if the elevation of 6700 feet has already got you huffing and puffing. In addition, all the quaint little *callejones*, that seem so enchanting when you first walk around the town, become rushing cascades when a good rain hits, so bring an extra pair of shoes if you are going to be there during the rainy season.

Tlaxcala

If you are looking for a smaller city with lots of charm, Tlaxcala is hard to beat (Man, that sounds schlocky, doesn't it). It is a truly lovely colonial city that is easy to get around and only about 50 minutes by bus from Puebla. Tlaxcala is a city of history and traditions, so there is much to see in terms of historical buildings, such as the country's oldest bullfighting ring and the lovely Basilica de Nuestra Señora de Ocotlán.

Most will agree that the food in Tlaxcala is very good, and it in fact makes claims to being the home of not only *mole* (Poblanos do not agree) and *tacos de canasta,* but even of the tortilla itself, a fact you will even see in the city's seal. Tlaxcala is especially well known for the production of *pulque,* that somewhat viscous fermented beverage which was once the staple of the working class (before the beer companies came in and played dirty). At any rate, if you have never tried fresh pulque (not the junk in a can), you are in for a treat! Tía Yola's right off the lovely Plaza Xicotencatl, one of the two plazas at the heart of the city, is a great and comfortable place to give it a try. Try one of their *mixiote* dishes too, if you're hungry.

As for downsides, Tlaxcala is pretty high in elevation at 7345 feet, so you might get winded when first walking around. High elevation also means lower winter temps, which is a turn off for some, but then those altitudes generally mean cooler summer temps, so it is not all bad living up closer to the sky.

Zacatecas

While on the topic of high-altitude cities, Zacatecas is right up there at 8005 feet, and thus the same caveats mentioned for Tlaxcala hold true for Zacatecas. But jumping to the positive side of things, Zacatecas has a lot going for it. Many compare Zacatecas to Guanajuato in terms of its origins and thus its look and feel. A former mining town, like Guanajuato, it was once flush with cash, and that means it is full of beautiful architecture, much of which was made of local *cantera* stone, which has a pretty and soothing orangey pink color to it.

The city is also flush with museums that are all well worth seeing, especially the Rafael Colonel Museum which houses the biggest collection of masks you will probably ever see in one place, all located in a beautiful former convent. The city also boasts a very good food scene with a lot of European-esque bistros (Check out Mykonos and Lucky Luciano), and simple eateries with fare such as *tacos envenados* (poisoned tacos), the delicious little tortas from Tortas Malpaso in nearby Villanueva, and what could probably be called the city's signature dish, *Asado de Boda*. Oh, and if you are into such things, Zacatecas is also known for being one of the designated regions for mezcal production.

Oaxaca

You might be surprised to see me recommend Oaxaca as a place to live when I described it earlier as a place that disappointed me when I moved there. Well, even though it did disappoint me, I didn't think it was a bad place, and I know from experience that it is an easy place to live. That is probably why so many expats move and feel very happy there. As I mentioned earlier, one of Oaxaca's biggest draws is its food scene, as there are numerous great eateries in town, both local Mexican and European. The delicatessen/brew pub, Gourmand, is a great place, as is the very, almost excessively, popular bakery/restaurant, Boulanc. For Mexican fare with a great ambiance (and view!), nothing beats a rooftop meal at Pitiona or Casa Oaxaca.

Oaxaca also has lots of museums, workshops in

everything from embroidery to cheese making, and free classical concerts at the Teatro Macedonio de Alcalá. As I mentioned in an earlier chapter, the city also boasts some great amenities for expats, such as its Oaxaca Lending Library and Holy Trinity Anglican Church, and it has some good Spanish language schools.

On the down side, Oaxaca is a much poorer city than most of its colonial neighbors to the north, so some of it can look a bit tattered, with sidewalks here and there being in a very poor state of repair. Of course, for some, that is part of the city's charm. Oaxaca also has a very powerful and active teachers union that conducts rather big protests quite often. These protests, or *manifestaciones*, often include *bloqueos* (blockades) of major roads or highway toll booths and thus can shut down the city for long periods at a time. This can make the city, already rather geographically isolated from the rest of the country, feel even more isolated.

Of course, only you will know for sure if it is the place for you, so go check it out if it sounds as if it might have potential.

Mexico City

It's interesting to me that so many people omit Mexico City from their list of possible places to retire. It is even more surprising that many choose to omit it from their list of places to visit, which is a real pity since, as I mentioned earlier in the book, it has so much to offer.

Of course, rent wise, Mexico City will be more expensive than other cities, but for a city its size and grandeur, it is relatively cheap in the global scheme of things. I mean, most people could never envision retiring in New York City or London as the costs would be just too high. They are, after all, already too high for people who work and live in those cities! Mexico City, on the other hand, is doable if you look around. . .and have a bit more padding in your bank account.

I've already mentioned some of the plus points the

city has to offer, but there are also so many other diversions, including everything from *Lucha Libre* (Mexican style professional wrestling shows) to shopping and dining out (We love the great options for Korean food!). Public transportation is also plentiful and very reasonably priced, so you can really get anywhere you want in Mexico City without having to own or rent a car. Neighborhoods are varied and distinct, with Condesa and Roma Sur being very popular locations that feel almost like neighborhoods in Paris. Polanco is also popular, but it is a much pricier area, populated as it is with the embassy and big international corporation employee set.

All that said, I think it is worth at least considering Mexico City as a potential place to retire if it is within your budget. If nothing else, it is worth a look see to find out if does anything for you one way or the other.

A Few Others

There are plenty of other spots that I think are worthy of considering, though they don't exactly match my personal list of needs and prohibitions. **Puebla**, for example, is well worth considering. It has good temperatures, great food, and lots of big city amenities without being too big a city. To me, it's only downside is traffic, as there is no offstreet transportion options.

If you are a beach type person, which I am not, at least not for living purposes, you might consider **Mazatlán**. Mazatlán has a lovely colonial old town, an interesting and diverse history, and a well established, but not overwhelming, expat population. The good seafood and the region's excellent style of regional cooking in general are also attractions to the place, as are the lovely towns and villages in the mountains just away from the city, such as the postcard-pretty town of El Quelite. Oh, and if the plan to extend the El Chepe train from Los Mochis to Mazatlán actually comes to fruition, well, there will be that perk for you too.

Finally, there is **Ensenada**, which was one of the early expat retirement destinations. In fact, it was the second place I visited as a kid (Tijuana being the first). It is not a beautiful city *per se,* and the beach is not so much a beach as much as a functioning oceanfront, but there is good food, good weather, and easy living to be found. The area around Ensenada has become a pretty well-respected wine producing region too, so winery visits are now a thing to do, if you're into that. Yes, there is more to Ensenada than Hussongs Cantina!

For a beach town, the prices for rents and such are relatively reasonable, which is a definite plus. In addition, living in Ensenada puts you pretty close to the US border, thus making it is a good spot if you want to live in Mexico but depend on Medicare back home for major and catastrophic illnesses and incidents, etc. Because of that close proximity to the border, many expats in Ensenada tend to bring down or buy cars with which to make trips back home and explorations of the area easier. If you do end up doing that, be sure to apply for a US Sentri pass so as to dramatically cut down your border crossing times when heading back to the US.

My Thumbs-Down Locations

So there was my list of suggestions for places to consider moving to. There are lots of other places that you might find on your own or through recommendations from others, so my list is not exhaustive. It is just some suggestions to consider.

There are, however, some places that I advise against, based again on my own personal experiences. Again, your feelings or opinions might differ, and many people's do, so don't take these disadvisements as gospel. I offer them just so you hear a different take than the usual gush of positives that you will so often come across. Again, don't get me wrong; I am not presenting a list of dreadfully awful places at all. As I just implied, many people find some of them quite nice. What I am saying, however, is that if you are considering them for mid- to long-term living, well, here is what I've got to say about them. . .and you are free and welcome to ignore me.

Cuernavaca

I have very mixed feelings about Cuernavaca. On the one hand, we lived there about half a year and didn't have a miserable time of it. Our apartment was a reasonably priced unit with swimming pool and ping pong table. We enjoyed the Lebanese food that was pretty easy to find around town due to immigration from Lebanon at the turn of the previous century, and we loved the Italian restaurant Marco Polo, located in Centro right across from the Cathedral. There were some pretty nice sights to see, and being only an hour away from Mexico City was a pretty nice perk too. Oh, and the supermarkets are top notch!

No, Cuernavaca is not a bad place, but it is not the garden city that some people make it out to be. They call it the city of eternal spring, but for us it felt like the city of eternal summer as it was so often quite hot. It seems like a place that time has forgotten in that so much of the town looks run down. Obviously, Cuernavaca is a place that has seen better days.

There is a fair sized expat community in the city, but unless you go to the Episcopalian church there, you are unlikely to see any of those expats because they seem to live in walled-off homes and are driven around town by private drivers. All in all, it just felt a sort of off place. Don't shy away from it for a visit, but definitely give it a visit before you decide to move there.

Taxco

Taxco in the State of Guerrero is a lovely place to visit. It's a city of winding, hilly streets plied by white Volkswagen bug taxis making their way through a sea of chalk white colonial buildings. It definitely makes for a lovely postcard like settting.

The problem is that Taxco is sort of small, so a few hours is enough to take it all in, see more silver jewelry shops than you would ever want to see in a lifetime, have an average tasting lunch, and sit around for a while to relax. Thus, the notion of living there seems like an invitation to madness through monotony and boredom. Definitely do a day trip there, but I wouldn't waste too much time thinking about living there.

Cholula

Now this is a place that I really don't get at all, even for a visit, and yet many people love it. My objections to Cholula are many, but the first is that it is too near Puebla, so near, in fact, that it is hard to tell where one city ends and the other begins. And despite being so near, it is somehow sort of a hassle to get to it, and once you do get to it, there isn't very much to see.

The big attraction in Cholula is the Great Pyramid of Cholula, or *Tlachihualtepetl,* which is touted as the largest pyramid (in volume) in the world. Of course, you would never know to look at it since it just looks like an out of place mountain.

The pyramid does have a sort of interesting history in that it was built by one ancient culture, and then built over by five successive cultures that came to dominate the area through time. To cap it all off, quite literally, when the Spanish arrived in Mexico and made their presence known, the locals took to burying the then out-of-use and grown-over pyramid, thereby turning the thing into the big mountain you see today. When the Spanish finally came to town permanently, they topped it all off with a church, the *Iglesia de Nuestra Señora de los Remedios.*

The rite of touristic passage in Cholula seems to be climbing the covered pyramid to the church up on top so, I assume, that you can brag you made it up there, which is quite a feat given the already high altitude you start at. Oh well. To each his own.

Beyond that, there isn't really much to see or do. Again, there are many who must see something that I just don't because they rave about Cholula and even choose to move to the place. That all said, go see for yourself, but, as I've said for other locations, don't even think about moving there until you've visited the place.

Querétaro

The thing that I've always found odd about Querétaro is that so many Mexicans speak so highly of it, as if it some sort of dream city to move to. They say it is safe and clean and, as one acquaintance said, "future oriented." Many expats love it too because they too say it is so clean and easy to live in. We went there, even took a tour, and it seemed quite adequate, but essentially unimpressive...dull. And I don't think it seemed any cleaner than the next city. The historic downtown area was OK, but sort of thin when compared to other colonial cities nearby, like Guanajuato or San Miguel de Allende. Outside of the Centro area, the place sort of savored of. . . suburban Los Angeles, which might be why, I reckon, that some expats like it.

The only thing we saw in our time there that was even remotely interesting was a statue of Junipero Serra (That's right, the California missions guy), not that I am particularly interested in him *per se,* but in an era in which people are tearing statues of him down back home, finding a statue of him standing there without any graffitti or other form of protest defacement was a surprize. As I had always associated the guy with California (and elementary school field trips to the missions there), I was confused as to what he was doing there down in Querétaro. As it turns out, Fr. Serra had been busy establishing missions in the State of Querétaro before he set off to Alta California to subjugate the locals there.

OK, so that was sort of interesting, but not enough to raise our impression of the city. We remained as nonplussed by the place when we left as when we arrived. Then again, we were not looking at the place through the eyes of future residents but rather though the eyes of tourists, so that might have skewed our reaction. Again, we are in the minority, it seems, when it comes to our view of Querétaro, so if you are interested, go look and see, and decide for yourself.

CHAPTER 12: FINDING AN APARTMENT

Finding a place to live in, an apartment or house, is one of the most stressful parts of moving to a new place, whether it is in another city in your own country or in a foreign country. The latter case is all the harder because you have so many things to overcome. Not only do you have to worry about language barriers but also about renting customs. On top of that, just deciding what part of town of the city to settle upon is a challenge since you lack that local familiarity that benefits you when looking for a place in your own city back home.

This last point is one of the reasons that I, and so many others, strongly advise against buying a place to live until you are familiar with the city or town in which you are planning to live and how things vary during the night vs during the day. Nothing worse than buying a house and then discovering six months later that you really wish you had bought a place on the other side of town. And then there is the case of buying your house in City X, only to find that you wish you had decided on moving to City Z after visiting it.

With renting, you can afford to make mistakes. If you don't like where you chose, you will be able to move later without too much fuss, whether it be to a different area in the same city or to a different city altogether... or maybe even back home if you find that Mexico is not all you expected it to be.

Pets

Let's start things off by talking about renting with pets, since it is something expats-to-be often ask about. Yes, you can rent an apartment that will allow pets, but your choices will be reduced greatly. Interestingly, it is easier to find a place that will accept a dog than it is to find one that will accept a cat. Either way, if you wish to bring your sweet and furry friend with you to Mexico, as we did, just be aware that the going will be a tad rougher than if you go petless.

How Much To Expect In Rent

Rents can be all over the place depending on size, location, amenities, and so on. I remember asking the same question to my online Spanish teacher before I moved to Mexico, and he said "It depends on so many things. Do you want a garden or no garden. Near Centro or not near Centro. Uphill or in the flat areas. Pets or no pets. Furnished or unfurnished. One room or more rooms. Utilities included or not. And so on." That all said, you can expect anything from $250 for a small and basic place to $1000 in the normal range, and even more if you are in a resort area or dealing with one of those realtors from the show Househunters International. Expect any rentals you find on AirBnB or from an expat-oriented service to be higher than from a Mexican traditional source. The best way to get a good idea of what your range is going to be is to ask around in online groups that are specific to the area you are interested in.

How To Find A Place

Used to be savvy expats would give pretty much the same advice when asked by newbies how to find an apartment. Basically the method was two-fold. First, map out areas of town you are interested in, and walk all around them, looking for *Se Renta* (For Rent) signs in the windows. Having a native call up for you was usually also suggested so as to avoid the landlord trying jack up the rent for a rich foreigner. The second part of the program consisted of spreading the word that you were looking for a place to rent. Tell, the taxi driver, tell the woman at the papelería, tell counter workers at the local store. The idea being that if you spread the word, you might get some bites.

I tried these methods in both Guanajuato and Oaxaca with varying degrees of success. In Guanajuato, people were telling me prior to arrival that finding a place for $200-$350 a month would be easy as pie. Once I got there, though, all those advisors suddenly switched gears saying things like "oh, you want an apartment, not a room," or other such responses. In Guanajuato, I only saw a total of three *Se Renta* signs the whole time I was there, and two of those were for rooms, while one was for a store front. In Oaxaca, I was more successful, but just barely. I did find a few *Se Renta* signs there, and I actually checked out two of them that seemed to be in an area that would be good for me.

The first was overpriced at $700 a month and a bit of a wreck, while the second was more reasonable but reeked of bug spray and seemed to have some plumbing problems, which led me to just keep on looking. I also got a bite via the spread-the-word method. While spreading the word, I stopped at an AirBnB I had stayed at previously during my first visit to the city to see if they had any long-term openings and, if not, to ask them to spread the word. A week later, I got a call from the girl who worked there saying that she had found an apartment that was reasonably priced and convenient to town. Well, all things were relative since the place was in a very odd part of town that was quite inconvenient to get to and from, and the place was completely unfurnished with not so much as a towel rack inside. Utilities were also not included. I was very grateful for the effort and the find, but I had to decline. That led, it certainly seemed, to some hard feelings coming my way. I thus learned that putting out the word can have repercussions.

Nonetheless, it is clear that there is some sense in the old advice, so don't ignore it in favor of the more current methods that I will cover next. The old ways might work for you, so they are definitely worth a try.

AirBnB

One of the most popular ways to find a place to live these days, especially for expats, is through AirBnB. It is an easy and familiar process, after all, and you can find a place for either short or long stays. You can do everything online before you even arrive in the country, and you'll know what it will cost you from day one. The offerings are varied in type and in location, and some of the rentals are quite interesting.

Of course, paying daily rates would not be sustainable long term, but many units offer significant rate reductions for longer rentals. I found four apartments in this way in Mexico, though one of them did not offer long term rate reductions, so that one ended up being used for a short stay only. It is worth mentioning here another advantage of AirBnB: it is easier to find rentals that will accept pets. Just use the pets-OK filter in your search, and you can save yourself a lot of grief and wasted time.

AirBnB is all fine and dandy, but the AirBnB boom has had the ironic side effect of making regular rentals harder to find. The more landlords go the AirBnB route, the fewer traditional rentals there will be. I can say that I have witnessed this happen while in Guanajuato, where two different Spanish teachers of mine suddenly had to search for new places to live because their landlords had decided to go the AirBnB route. Of course, they had the option of staying, albeit at the new greatly increased rent. They thus both declined.

Business wise, I suppose it makes sense. Why rent out a unit to locals for $300 a month when you can rent it out to well heeled foreign or Mexico City tourists for twice as much or more? Still as we all know from the American example, problems of rental affordability and availability invariably come to play as the phenomenon grows. Abracadabra! Gentrification before our eyes!

Vivanuncios

AirBnB is not the only game in town when it comes to looking for rentals online. Probably the most popular Mexican site is one called Vivanuncios (www.vivanuncios.com.mx). It is more of a traditional real estate site, somewhat like Zillow or Trulia, that covers both home sales and rentals rather than short-term rentals, as is the main focus on AirBnB. The site is all in Spanish, but it is pretty easy to figure out. Remember that prices are given in Pesos, not dollars. People sometimes panic when they first see the prices because they interpret the dollar sign ($) to mean dollars, whereas in the Mexican context it also means pesos.

I actually found my first regular rental in Oaxaca via Vivanuncios. Well, actually, I found a lower rent for my apartment on Vivanuncios. I originally found the apartment in the Apartments For Rent listing notebook at the Oaxaca Lending Library, one of their many services. The rent in the notebook flyer was $600 a month, which was over my budget and thus why I had originally ignored the flyer when I first saw it. Imagine my surprise when, a couple weeks later, I find an ad for the same apartment (this time in Spanish) on Vivanuncios but for $150 dollars less. Though 50 dollars more than I wanted to pay, it was the best thing I had come up with so far, and since my AirBnB short-term rental was going to be over soon, and someone else was scheduled to be moving in, I really needed to get out ASAP, so I called in saying I had seen the ad in Vivanuncios, and got the apartment for the lesser rent.

That was my first experience, at least conspicuous experience, with what they call the "gringo tax." The irony, however, was that the apartment was actually owned by a Slovak woman, so it was all a sort of a case of gringos overcharging gringos in action. Wow.

Expect The Unexpected

While we are on the topic of that Oaxaca apartment, let's jump to a warning based on my experience there: Expect the unexpected! You see that Oaxaca apartment story is not over. After making contact via Vivanuncios, I met the agent handling the rental of the apartment near the apartment itself. He was a nice fellow and very helpful. I confirmed the rent first of all, and he confirmed the Vivanuncios price. I then told him I had a cat and asked if that would be acceptable. He said, of course, "in fact, part of your responsibilities is to feed the stray cats downstairs at the apartment."

Wuh?? I love cats and all, but why would I have to take care of strays? It just seemed weird to me, but I was so glad to have found a decent place that accepted cats at a somewhat affordable price that I kept my mouth shut. On moving day, the agent was even kind enough to drive to my AirBnB and transport me, all my stuff, and my cat to the new place.

Everything seemed fine enough, but I was getting tired of the giant spiders crawling out of the walls, the neverending lines of ants that seemed to come out of nowhere, and the cawing from what seemed to be a vulture's nest in the wood down across a small valley from the veranda. The interior furnishings were nice enough, but the throw rug had a non-slip foam backing that was deteriorating due to age and thus leaving a mess, so I rolled it up and placed it in the storage room off of the kitchen.

It was not a perfect place, but it was fine enough for the time being, so I put up with whatever was not quite up to snuff. Then one day, my cat got out and went on a walkabout, making her way over the roof and into the garden of the house next door. That house was, it turned out, owned and occupied by the sister of the owner of the apartment I was renting.

As fate would have it, my landlord was visiting her sis that day and thus witnessed the visitation of my kitty. A couple of days later, she gave me a call. She complained because I had a cat, and no cats were allowed. She then complained that I had removed the throw rug, which means that she had visited the apartment when I was not there. Long story short, within one month of my moving in, I was told I had to move out. The landlord, in another slightly grating moment, only gave me 80% of my deposit back, docking the other 20% for the replacement of the toilet, which she said I had broken, despite my having mentioned the broken toilet to the agent when I first looked at the place.

Well, not all surprises are that weird or problematic, but one never knows what might come up. Some people have discovered that their neighbors have barking dogs that spend the night exercising their vocal powers. Others discover that the quiet cafe down the street during the day turns into a bar at night and blasts music at full volume until well after 3AM. One of my short-term rentals in Guanajuato, I learned on my first night, was on the same *callejón* as a drummer, who seemed especially keen on practicing late at night, with the tight little *callejón* providing excellent echo power.

Sometimes it is not outside problems that are the surprise. Often it is just the way apartments are that surprises. Whether it be that an unfurnished apartment can mean completely unfurnished down to the light fixtures, or that in many areas window screens are, well, not a thing, there are always surprises awaiting. That all said, when looking for a place in which to live, see what your apartment already has and what you are going to need to buy for it. Also try to visit the immediate neighborhood not only during the day but also at night to see if there is anything thing going on at night that would make you not want to live there.

The Rental Process

Once you've decided upon your apartment, the process to procure it is not much different than in most countries. You sign a contract, pay first and last month's rent up front, with the last month's rent being the security deposit. Be sure to learn clearly when each month's rent is due by and in which manner. Sometimes they might want you to pay in cash, sometimes via bank transfer. Of course, if you are renting via AirBnB, it is all handled online.

Sometimes a landlord will want you to have a Mexican guarantor, *fiador*, who will vouch to pay for any damage you do to the place. Such a guarantor has to actually own property in the same city as the rental, with their property standing as collateral for any damages or lawsuits that you are responsible for but cannot pay for. Needless to say, it can be tough for you to find a guarantor, especially when new to the country.

Fortunately, this is not a universal requirement, and is usually only true in bigger cities in more corporately run type buildings. In many cases, you can get away without having a guarantor by just offering to pay a larger deposit.

Any Tips For A Newly Arrive Renter-To-Be?

Well, yes. First thing, as I have said many times in the book, is to figure out what city and what part of the city you want to live in. Once that is done, find something with utilities included and that is furnished. This will give you time to get to know the city and get used to functioning in a Mexican environment before you have to go around dealing with buying furniture, getting window blinds, setting up utility accounts, and other things that might prove a tad overwhelming to a newcomer. I mean, just getting your first cellphone plan is enough of a challenge at first, so don't push yourself into the arms of stress. That said, starting off in an AirBnB rental for a few months, might not be a bad way to start off your life in Mexico. If you later decide to move to a cheaper or bigger or more *you* place, you will by then be better familiar with your city, better connected, and better able emotionally and linguistically to sweat the other stuff that comes up.

CHAPTER 13: MONEY MATTERS

For whatever reason you find yourself in Mexico, money is something you can't avoid worrying about, even if it is just in the sense of how to handle it. From how to get your money while in Mexico to how to convert it to pesos, your existence in Mexico is dependent on money handling. Fortunately, it is not at all difficult on the Mexican side of things, so take heart.

Introducing The CURP

Before moving any further, let me introduce you to a word that will prove very important to you if you become a resident in Mexico, and that word is *CURP*. CURP is an acronym that stands for *Clave Única de Registro de Población*, which means *Unique Population Registration Code*. (Talk about telling it like it is!).

Every Mexican citizen and official resident has a CURP, which is a unique identifier that is shared by no one else. In that sense, you can think of it as the Mexican equivalent of a US Social Security number (SNN), and like an SSN, it is required for many things, including opening a bank account, buying and registering a car, etc. Unlike an SSN, however, the CURP is a combination of letters and numbers, and it is much longer, consisting of 18 alphanumeric characters in contrast to the SSN's ten. You can find your CURP on your residency card when you get it.

In fact, the interesting thing about a CURP is that, while it is unique, it is not random in its generation. It is based, at least partially, on the holder's personal information, such as his/her name and date of birth. There is a pattern to the CURP. If you're interested, this is what it is:

1. First letter of the paternal surname.
2. First internal vowel of the paternal surname.
3. First letter of the maternal surname.
4. First letter of the holder's first name.
5. Date of birth in YY/MO/DAY format.
6. The holder's gender - *(H* for *Hombre* or *M* for *Mujer)*
7. Two-letter identifier for the Mexican state of birth.
8. First internal consonant of paternal surname.
9. First internal consonant of maternal surname.
10. First internal consonant of holder's first name.

For those born abroad, *NE* (for *Nacido en el Extranjero*, meaning *born abroad*) is used in place of the Mexican state identifier. In addition, *X* is used in place of any of those items dependent on the mother's maiden name in CURPs for foreigners

After all that comes a number or letter to help differentiate people with similar information. For those born before 2000, it will be a number between 0 and 9, and for those born after it will be a letter A-Z. Finally, there will be a number 0-9 at the end which acts as a checksum.

So. let's say we have a woman by the name of Blaza Sierra Hernandez, born on May 16, 1944 in Phoenix, Arizona. Her CURP would be SIHB440516MNERRL. . . plus the unique identifier, which would be a number between 0=9 in this case, and a checksum number. Fun, huh?

Well, OK, so you certainly do not need to know any of that information on the makeup of a CURP, but it is sort of interesting, no? Call me a nerd at heart, I guess.

Banking Through A Bank In Mexico

In your online wanderings in Mexico online groups, you will find that many people ask how or where to open a bank account, and others often respond by asking why on earth anyone would want to do that. Those two viewpoints should tell you something right there: you can open a bank account in Mexico, but you can usually get by without one.

In general, anyone with residency can open a bank account. Yes, there are some banks that will only open accounts for those with permanent residency, but most will open to anyone who has a CURP. When looking for a bank, it pays to shop around because not all banks are as easy to deal with. Some have rather high minimum deposit amounts, while some actually charge you a rather hefty fee, between 1000 to 3000 pesos to just open an account.

There are many banks in Mexico, of course, though which ones will have branches near you depends on where you live. Some of the big Mexican banks are Santander, BBVA, Scotiabank, Banorte, HBSC, and Banco Azteca, among others. Many expats recommend Intercam, as they do not have fees and seem to give no grief, so you can check them out also if there is one in your area.

Banking Through Your Bank Back Home

Those who choose not to open a Mexican bank account, just use their bank account back home, assuming they still have one. Their income, either from digital/online work, pension or Social Security payments, or from investments, etc., is already going into the account anyway, so why bother with a Mexican account goes the logic.

Going this route is easy enough, as you can just go to a local Mexican bank and use their ATM to withdraw funds as pesos with which to do all you have to do in Mexico. Yes, there are fees charged for the international transaction and for the conversion fee, but if you limit the frequency of withdrawals, meaning taking out a week or two's worth of pesos at a tme, you can keep those fees to a minimum. In other words, don't use your ATM card from your bank back home as a way to pay for things on a daily basis. Instead, use it to get cash once in a while, and then live on that.

Many expats like to avoid fees altogether and thus use, and recommend others use, a Charles Schwab account. With a Charles Schwab account, all international fees are refunded to you, which is nice. Charles Schwab accounts, however, are designed for Americans travelling abroad, so they require that you have a real US address. Also potentially worrisome is that if Charles Schwab determines, through your card's continued usage abroad, that you actually live abroad rather than in the US, they can shut down your account. It is also worth noting that they also require a credit check before an account can be opened, so bear that all in mind if you are thinking of going the Charles Schwab route.

Getting Pesos From A Mexican ATM

You don't have to have a bank account in Mexico to use their ATMs. As I mentioned in the previous section, people who do all their banking from an account back home, function in Mexico by withdrawing their money from an ATM at a Mexican bank. Of course, if you are just a tourist, this is natural enough since you sure aren't going to open a bank account for a short term stay.

You're not allowed to anyway. And so, your Mexican ATM is your friend.

There are a couple of things to know when using a Mexican ATM. First of all, there is usually a button offering you a choice of languages, Spanish or English. On some ATMs, all choices are written out in Spanish and English, so there will be no need to make a choice. So that said, you will have no problems language wise using an ATM in Mexico.

Another point is that there will be limits on how much money you can withdraw from an ATM at one time and even during the same day, just as is usually the case back home. You should check on this with the banks you are thinking of using. Remember also that some banks charge more than others for international fees and currency exchange transactions, so it is useful to ask around and see what banks in your area offer the best rates.

Finally, almost everyone you meet, online or in person, will tell you the same thing. When you withdraw money from an ATM, after selecting the peso amount you want to withdraw, a screen will appear offering you an exchange rate for that transaction. Everyone advises you to decline the rate because it is almost always a worse rate than the current market rate, which is what you will get if you decline the offer. I have found the advice to be true in my experiences, so if you want to save a few bucks here and there, try doing the same.

Don't Forget To Let Your Bank Know You Are Abroad

One thing that you need to be sure to do before heading off to Mexico, either to live or just to visit, is to let your bank know you will be travelling to Mexico and from when to when. There is nothing more nervewracking than trying to get some money out of an ATM in Mexico and your request being denied by your bank back home. If the bank doesn't know you are in Mexico, they may mark your transactions there as suspicious activity, and thus deny them until they can contact you or you can contact them to rectify the situation. For that reason, it is also very important that the bank has your current email address and telephone number in case they try to contact you if they see charges that raise their suspicions.

Social Security

Expats-to-be often worry that they will not be able to receive Social Security if they move abroad. That is essentially incorrect. You can get regular retirement Social Security wherever you live. You paid for it, so it is yours. My great uncle worked until retirement in the US, and then moved back to the former Yugoslavia where he could, using his words, "live like a king" on his Social Security, and for the most part he was right. The same is true for SSDI, Social Security Disability Insurance. The exception to all this is SSI, or Supplemental Security Income. You will lose SSI if you move abroad.

Finally, if you have a Mexican bank account, Social Security can arrange for your deposits to go directly into your Mexican account. Many expats do this while many others advise against it, their main objection being that you are stuck to the exchange rate in play the day that the deposit is made. If your deposits are made into a bank account in the US, you can decide when to move the money over, thus giving you some control of exchange rates. If you are interested in direct deposit into your account in Mexico, contact the Federal Benefits Unit at the Embassy or consulate that has jurisdiction over your state within Mexico. There are three such units in Mexico, one at the US Consulate in Ciuadad Juárez, Chihuahua, which handles the northern border states; the US Consulate in Guadalajara, which has jurisdiction over the States in western Central Mexico (Baja Sur, Sinaloa, Durango, Nayarit, Zacatecas, Aguascalientes, and Jalisco); and then the US Embassy in Mexico City, which has jurisdiction over the rest of the country.

NOTE: Be aware that if you are a Social Security retirement recipient abroad, Social Security will send you a letter every two years by which to make sure that you are still alive and that your payments are not falling into someone else's hands. If the letter is sent out, and you do not respond, Social Security will stop payments to you until your rectify the situation. Given the dicey nature of Mexico's mail system, this is a worrisome thing, so be on your guard and make sure Social Security has an address where you can receive mail.

Tipping

Many people think of Mexico as a no-tipping-necessary country. Well, no tip is required, but that does not mean that people do not tip at all. People tip (sit-down) restaurant servers, beauticians and barbers, taxi drivers, airport porters, hotel bellhops, and, as you will learn in the upcoming chapter on Shopping, even the baggers at the grocery checkout counter.

The question, therefore, is not whether or not you should tip (It is strictly up to you and whether or not the tip is deserved), but rather how much you should tip. For restaurants, tips of 10 to 15% are quite reasonable. As for tips for porters, bellhops, and taxi drivers, tip as you normally would back home, albeit in keeping with the cost of living in Mexico. In the case of taxi drivers, it is not unusual to tip them a bit more if they are helping you to unload your groceries or purchases after a shopping trip.

CHAPTER 14: HEALTH MATTERS

Regardless of your age, your health always has a way of reminding you that it's there and in need of care. The problem is that it tends to remind you at the worst possible times. A cavity or a chipped tooth can happen to you anywhere and at any time, whether you are seventeen or seventy. Broken bones are the reserve of no one group, and can happen while on the ski slope or while just crossing the street. Ah, and colds, flus, and whatever else nature has in season to throw out at you, are all equal opportunity in nature. For this reason, health matters is a subject area well worth examining so that you are at least prepared should something befall you in that area. It is also an area that many expats worry about, especially when it comes to health insurance.

Before You Go

It is always a good idea to make sure your own health house is in order before going off on any international adventure, a point some folks neglect when heading to Mexico, no doubt because it is so close that one is lulled into forgetting the foreign aspect of the place. It is always good to be up to date on your standard vaccinations and check with your doctor or the CDC to see if there are any vaccinations recommended for travel to Mexico at that time. You will probably find that the two usually recommended are Hepatitis A and Typhoid. There is no need for most people to get a physical just for the trip, but if something is ailing you, then get it looked at before you go so that it doesn't come and nip you when you would least want it to. The CDC has a whole page of potential health and other issues you might face in Mexico on its CDC Yellow Book page for Mexico.

Dentists

Rather than starting with bodily health problems in Mexico, let's start with your teeth since dental problems are one of the most common problems a traveler or expat might face. I remember the evening I arrived in Seattle at the age of 24, a horrendous toothache came hitting out of the blue, necessitating a desperate search for and visit to a dentist. Not exactly how I wanted to spend the first night and my next day in Seattle, but that is how it goes.

If you find yourself in such a dental fix while in Mexico, you can consider yourself lucky because Mexico is flush with dentists, and lots and lots of good ones at that. Dentistry in Mexico is also much cheaper than it is back home, which is often ridiculously overpriced. For example, I got a new ceramic crown in Mexico that cost $900 less than what was quoted to me in the US, and yet the work, both of the dentist and the dental tech who made the crown was excellent.

Just because a new crown and its installation is cheaper does not mean that it is not as good as what you get back home. I mean a crown on its own is not really that expensive a thing. I had a friend back in North Carolina who was a dental tech. He said that the price they charged dentists for a crown was about $90-$150 US. The dentists, of course, charge the customer ten times that. So a lot of that difference pays for the labor in the dentist office. . .and the office rent.

Of course, just as back home there are excellent dentists and those that are. . .well, not, so it is in Mexico. So it always behooves you to ask around for recommendations for a good one. Online groups for the area you are living in, or local expat services, such as expat clubs or libraries or churches, are great places to ask.

Doctors

As it is the case with dentists in Mexico, so it is with doctors. Mexico has lots of excellent, well-trained doctors, and as is also the case with dentists, a visit to the doctor is not a break-the-bank endeavor as it can be in the US. In my own experience, my doctor visits in Mexico have been less expensive than my usual co-pays for doctors back home. Of course, your mileage may differ, but the point remains that a visit to the doctor can be, for many, if not most, expats, an affordable out-of-pocket expense.

Just as with dentists, doctors have different reputations and, if language is an issue, levels of English proficiency. That said, it is always good to get recommendations for doctors in the areas you are going to live. In fact, one of the first things you should do when you get settled in any city where you are going to spend some time is to solicit recommendations for a good dentist and doctor, get their contact information and address, and then keep that information in your wallet and on your refrigerator door so that you won't have to be fishing for such info when you actually need it.

Many doctors have their own private offices while others work in a large clinic or a hospital. In any of these cases, the processes are pretty much the same as in the US, albeit without the seemingly endless pile of pre-treatment paperwork. Generally speaking, you make your appointment, announce your arrival, see the doctor, and pay as you leave.

Pharmacies (And The Little Clinics Next To Them)

One thing that surprises many a newly arrived visitor to Mexico is that there are so many pharmacies. It seems in some areas that you are always within a five minute walk from one or two of them. What surprises newbies even more, however, is the fact that many of the prescriptions you have from back home do not require a prescription in Mexico. You can just go to the pharmacy with the name and dosage of the medication you need, and they will sell it to you just like that. . . and at a much lower price than the same medicine would cost back home (unless, of course, you have really good prescription med coverage back home, that is).

Some medications, of course, do require a subscription. These would include antibiotics, psychotropics (like sedatives and stimulants), and opiates. If you take some unusual or highly specialized drug, it is always a good idea to see if it is available in Mexico before you decide on moving there. Some drugs are not available in Mexico.

While on the topic of pharmacies, you will find that next to or within many pharmacies there is often a small clinic with a doctor. These are walk-up clinics, so no need for an appointment. The wait time for these clinics is usually short, and the prices very, very low. They are geared toward consultations for common problems like stomach aches, diarrhea, cold, flus, rashes and so on. The doctors in such clinics can write you prescriptions too. At any rate, these clinics are handy and convenient for minor ailments, so it is a good idea to be aware where the closest one to your home is and what its hours are. Think of it as a first line of defense.

Travellers Insurance

Let us now broach the topic of insurance by starting with travellers insurance. Travellers insurance is available only to those who will be going to Mexico for a limited period of time, which could be anything from a few days to six months. A lot of people go by the thinking that nothing is going to happen to them in that short a period of time, and if anything does, well, the doctors in Mexico are pretty cheap, so what's the point of throwing money away on travellers insurance. Well, it certainly is true that doctors in Mexico are cheap, but hospitalization and emergency services are not. As for the nothing is going to happen to you in such a short period of time notion, well, when it comes to travelling, problems can happen even before you get off the plane.

I remember a short-term student from China at the university where I used to work. Oh, did she have a tale of woe! She flew to the US for her short-term language program, excited about the adventure she was about to embark on. After the plane landed and people began deplaning, she began to feel dizzy, and . . . *bam*, she fell backward, hit her head on the ground, and passed out. After a trip in an ambulance to the ER, and a few hours recuperation, she was back to normal and off on her merry way, albeit slightly delayed. A month later and back in China, she was being hounded for payment of an enormously large medical bill. No, she did not have any travellers insurance. Ouch.

That said, even though the stats are with you that you will avoid a medical mishap on a short trip, if you are the 1 in 1000 who gets sick, or, worse yet, the 1 in 2000 who ends up requiring treatment in a hospital, having travellers insurance sure would give you some peace of mind and keep you from getting stuck in hospital until you come up with the money to pay your bill.

That, of course, is a personal decision, and everything we do in life is a gamble of sorts. Still, it is something to consider, and there are lots and lots of companies offering such travellers insurance policies. Nomad Insurance used to be a popular one among young Lonely Planet types, and I assume it still is. Then there are the big names like Allianz, Generali, and Travel Guard from AIG. You are sure to find more when you start searching or asking around. Costs of such policies vary by company, policy features, age of the traveler, and duration of stay, so for purposes of comparison, an insurance comparison site, such as Travel Insurance Master, can be very useful.

> **NOTE:** Travellers insurance is not designed to replace regular health insurance. While travellers insurance is fairly low cost and convenient, as it requires no medical exams or questionnaires to get, it is only offered short term and primarily only covers emergencies and accidents. It does not cover long-term conditions or provide health maintenance or preventative health coverage. In other words, travellers insurance is for travellers. It is not appropriate for those who plan to live in Mexico long-term, i.e, beyond a stay of 180 days.

Health Insurance

We now leave the topic of travellers insurance and switch to health insurance. Many mistakenly think of travellers insurance as a form of health insurance, but it is not. Unlike travellers insurance, health insurance not only covers medical emergencies, but also covers long-term conditions, and usually, depending on the provider and policy, provides coverage for preventative health and health maintenance. It is insurance for the long term, with coverage provisions essentially set for life at the time you join. It is more expensive, often requires a physical and/or medical history investigation, and the premiums do go up over time, but health insurance is really the only choice available for the long-term expat when it comes to the two types of insurance we are discussing.

That being the case, it is no surprise that health insurance is something that concerns every expat who moves to Mexico. After all, as you get older, the chance of needing medical care increases, and everyone who has looked into the subject knows the cost of insurance only goes up as you age. I hate to be a dream dasher yet again in my own book, but there is no silver bullet that solves this problem. The problems are real, and preparing for them is often a matter of assessing one's own state of affairs, making some choices and compromises, and then coming up with a plan that works for you.

An expat in Mexico basically has three options when it comes to health insurance: INSABI, IMSS, or private insurance. There are also some who choose to live close to the border and depend on making border crossings to use their Medicare back home, and then there are those who just go without any insurance, choosing instead to depend on savings to pay any medical costs out of pocket.

INSABI

Let us start examing these options by first looking at INSABI. I suppose one can take some solace in the fact that the minute you get your residency approved and you thus have that CURP number, printed right there on your residency card, you automatically become a member of INSABI (*Instituto Nacional de Salud para el Bienestar = Institute of Health for Welfare*). You don't have to join or apply; you are just in without any additional action on your part. All you have to do if you are in need of care is to go to a *Centro de Salud* (which is what INSABI clinics are called) with a printout of your CURP and, just in case, your residency card, and you will be good to go. Wait times should be relatively short if you are going for a primary care consultations, but it you need to see a specialist, be prepared for some probable lengthy waiting.

By the way, if you have ever run across the name *Seguro Popular* in your readings or conversations with Mexico savvy types, INSABI is its replacement. Basically, you can think of

INSABI, like Seguro Popular before it, as the base level of the health care system in Mexico. I guess that means you can consider it the country's healthcare safety net.

Some expats shy away from using the services of INSABI because they feel as if they are taking advantage of a system that was originally designed to care for Mexico's poor. They are also fear from what they have heard that the care is subpar or at least more rudimentary than they are accustomed to, particularly when it comes to hospitalization. While it is true that the system was designed for the poor, it is made available to all in Mexico. As for the quality of care and facilities, that really depends on where you are in Mexico, as such things can vary from place to place. At any rate, it should provide some comfort of mind for you to know that you have at least something insurance wise once you become a resident.

If you need to go to a Centro de Salud, you can get a printout of your CURP beforehand by going to this governmental site: https://www.gob.mx/curp/.

IMSS

Another public health insurance scheme available to resident expats in Mexico (i.e., those with a CURP) is IMSS (*Instituto Mexicano del Seguro Social = Mexican Social Security Institute*). Unlike INSABI, which is automatically available to anyone with a CURP, you must apply to become a member of IMSS, and you must pay for it annually based on your age, with rates growing higher as you grow older. For someone from the ages of 60 to 69, for example, that annual fee would be $18,300 MX, and it would work itself up to $19,700 MX once you hit 80, after which it remains at that same level. If you do the math and covert those annual fees, you'll see that while the fees are not exactly cheap, $1156 US for a annual premium for an 85 year old ain't bad.

So, as you can see, one reason expats want to join IMSS is because it is pretty reasonable in terms of cost. It is not as cheap as INSABI, which has no premiums, but still many people want to join IMSS because they consider it to be a better system than INSABI. Many will agree, but that really depends where you live and which facilities each system has in that location, as in some locations the INSABI facilities might actually be better than those of IMSS. Even more importantly, IMSS is a healthcare system that seems somewhat familiar to expats as it in some ways resembles, or seems to resemble, the well-known Kaiser-Permanente system back home, a fact that seems to provide some peace of mind for some folks.

What keeps many people away from IMSS, or rather out of it, is the fact that you are required to undergo a physical in order to join, and if they find that you have certain pre-existing conditions, you're not only not covered for those conditions, you're not even allowed to join the IMSS system! Other conditions won't prevent you from being accepted to the system, but they won't be covered. It is thus probably safe to say that the younger and healthier you are when applying, the better. A list of pre-existing conditions that will sink your chance of membership in IMSS or affect your coverage can be found online at:

> https://www.imss.gob.mx/derechoH/enfermedad-seguros-familia.

It is worth noting that both IMSS and INSABI have a few limitations that might be off-putting or deal breakers for an expat (and even native Mexicans). A big one is that it can take a long time to get an appointment with a specialist. The same is also true for the scheduling of surgeries, which can take months, sometimes over a year, to happen. A bigger problem for many is that when it comes to hospitalizations, neither system necessarily provides full-nursing services. Patients are expected to elicit help from family and friends in order to provide support and some of the non-medical services that one normally receives (and pays for) in a private hospital.

Private Health Insurance

In addition to the two public health insurance schemes open to expats, there is always the private insurance option, which many expats and Mexicans prefer. I should warn you up front that when it comes to recommendations from other expats, a lot of what you'll get recommended is not health insurance at all but travellers insurance, which, as I pointed out earlier, is not what a longer term expat wants or needs or even qualifies for. What you do want is a policy that will cover you in Mexico and pay the hospital directly, not reimburse you after you've paid the bill up front. I mean unless you have a hundred thousand dollars lying around, the reimbursement route could leave you in a bad place.

Like health insurance back home, at least in the old days, pre-existing conditions are not covered. Some conditions, such as HIV or MS, can prevent you from being covered at all, while other conditions that are more common and manageable and not degenerative in nature, like high blood pressure, won't keep you from having insurance but won't be covered at all or only covered after the first year or more after starting membership. The scuttlebutt is that IMSS is much stricter in this regard, with some conditions considered minor by private insurers, like high blood pressure, being enough to prevent your from membership in the IMSS system. Your mileage, of course, may vary.

Another issue is that the older you get, the more expensive your premiums will become. This is similar to how things are with IMSS, but the difference there is that IMSS caps increases after the age of 80, after which the same rate holds true for the rest of your life, subject to overall rate increases in the system. On the other hand, private insurance premiums can just go up and up and up until you can't afford them anymore. In addition, some insurers will not insure you if you initially apply beyond a certain age, which can sometimes be as early as your mid to upper 60s. Definitely a couple of things to look out for when shopping for private insurance.

On the more positive side of things, private insurance means that you will be dealing with private doctors of your choice and with private hospitals with full services, so no need for you to arrange help from family or friends when you are in hospital. In addition, wait times for appointments with specialists and most operations or treatments will be far shorter than with the public hospitals, though prices will be more expensive.

There are lots of companies offering health insurance for Mexico, including big Mexican companies like GNP Seguros, Seguros Monterrey, and Metlife Mexico. Policies are also available from international insurers, such as Cigna, AXA, and VUMI.

Not only are there many companies, each of them offers many different policies and policy options, and thus finding the right package for your needs can be a real challenge and chore. It is thus a good idea to use an insurance broker who is familiar with the needs of expats in Mexico. One which is frequently recommended is Novamar Insurance, which not only handles health insurance, but also just about every other type of insurance that might be of use to you now or in the future - travellers, emergency medical evacuation, automobile, and even boat. If nothing else, they have an excellent site clarifying insurance types and special health insurance needs that expats have and should look out for.

Out of Pocket

It is a pretty common practice for expats and locals to pay for most office consultations and doctor services out of pocket. You get to go to the doctor you want, you don't have to endure long waits, and the costs are not very high, especially compared to what a doctor visit can cost back home, even with insurance.

Paying out of pocket for hospitalization and surgical procedures is more of a rarity. The reason is simple; hospital visits and/or surgery costs are significantly more than a visit to the doctor for treatment of a relatively minor ailment. Yes, hospital costs are far less in Mexico than they are in the US, but the hospitals can be very tough when it comes to making sure they get paid.

Private hospitals are known to require a deposit for most operations, and those deposits can be anywhere from from $5000 MXN to $100, 000 MXN. For elective procedures, they often make you pay in advance. The worst case scenario, and it does happen, is that at the completion of your treatment or surgery and recovery, the hospital will not let you leave until you've paid whatever is due on your bill. As some stays involving complicated surgeries can end up costing $90,000 US or more, you definitely want to make sure you have a lot of cash stashed away if you are going to depend on paying for your health care via the out-of-pocket route.

Medicare

If you have US Medicare, be aware that you cannot use it in Mexico except in vary rare and unusual circumstances. In general, you would have to fly or bus up to the US, and have whatever you need done at a facility in the US. And some people do just that, often choosing to live close to the border to facilitate the process. I even knew a fellow who lived in Coatepec, Veracruz, and took a bus up to his specialist in Texas twice to three times a year! I asked him if that wasn't a bit tiring, and he just said, "I'm retired! What else have I got to do?"

Well, fair enough, I had to admit, but I also know what it is like to cross into the US from Mexico by land. It can be a very time consuming and tiring experience. Crossing times, especially by car, can take hours! And sitting in the car that long, inching your way across is almost enough to drive you mad. Just imagine having to make that trip while truly ill and in need of hospital treatment.

Flying back home in such a situation is hardly any better as the whole proces of getting to the airport, waiting for and then boarding your plane, and then going through passport control on the other end is trying enough when you are healthy. Imagine doing all that when you're sick. On top of that, many airlines will not let you fly if you are in such bad shape. This is why many of those who use Medicare as their primary catastrophic insurance also buy a medical evacuation insurance policy, a topic I will touch upon in the next section.

Before going on to that, however, let me first give a bit of advice. Your Medicare coverage, as you no doubt know, consists of two parts: Part A, which covers hospital visits, and Part B, which covers doctor visits and outpatient services. You've paid for Part A through payroll deductions during your working life, so it is, after retirement, essentially free to you. Part B, on the other hand, is something you pay for each month, usually through a deduction from your Social Security payment. Currently, that monthly fee for Part B in 2024 is $174.70 US, which is a fair chunk of money, and that is why some people who move to Mexico decide to opt out of Part B, thinking that they can better use the money to save up for health coverage out of pocket or via private insurance in Mexico.

My advice is to not drop out until you have been in Mexico a few years and are absolutely sure you are going to stay there, or at least never live in the US again. If you drop out and then later decide to, or have to, move back to the US, you may face penalties or higher premium costs if you then re-enroll in Part B. I guess you can call this another example of the burn-no-bridges policy I always fall back on.

Emergency Medical Evacuation Insurance

Dire situations, like those I mentioned in the previous section on Medicare, are why many expats in Mexico decide to buy an emergency medical evacuation policy. Basically, what such a policy does is arrange and cover the costs of having you physically moved out of Mexico and back to the US to a hospital of your choice, which out of pocket would be a prohibitively expensive endeavor. Emergency medical evacuation policies are not cheap, with annual premiums in the $700 neighborhood not being uncommon, but that is a lot less than what an actual emergency medical evacuation from Mexico to the US would cost. Such an undertaking could easily cost somewhere in the upper five figure neighborhood (US Dollars). At any rate, emergency medical evacuation insurance is definitely something worth looking into as you decide what sort of insurance package your are going to set up for yourself. Medjet and Global Rescue are companies often mentioned, but there are others you can find through online searches or from recommendations in online forums or FB groups.

Food Safety

One of the Mexico's major attractions its cuisine. Unfortunately, many a visitor fails to enjoy the cuisine fully out of fear of getting sick. One can get sick simply because of eating food that is different in terms of contents than what they are familiar with. I mean, if you are not used to eating spicy food and suddenly start eating it, you might end up with some problems, at least initially. I know that *birria*, delicious as it might be, shoots right through me, necessitating my staying, ahem, close to home for a while. But that sort of reaction can happen anywhere, even back home. In that sense you are not really getting sick, you are just not intestinally acclimated. Don't eat things that cause you those problems, and you will be fine.

The real problem is with foods that have not been properly handled in some way, and thus make you sick due to contamination. This could happen at a restaurant or a food stand, so it is always important to be vigilant, but at the same time one can go a bit overboard and eat rather dull and boring food out of fear of getting sick. There is any number of ways to avoid this, and most are quite simple and commonsense.

Veggies And Fruit

First of all, avoid eating unpeeled fruit (strawberries and grapes, in particular) from street vendors unless you know that the fruit has been treated with an anti-bacterial solution. And if buying fruit in a cup from street vendors, stick to the peeled and cut fruits. Also avoid eating raw vegetables outside of home, and if eating them or fruits at home first treat them with *Microdyn.*

Microdyn is an iodine-based produce wash used to kill bacteria and/or bugs on your fruits and veggies. Just put a few drops in a tub of water and then soak your produce for 3 to 5 minutes. Of course, veggies and fruit with more cracks and crevices, such as broccoli or strawberries, might benefit from a bit longer soaking. Microdyn is sold in small plastic bottles that are usually found in the produce section of your supermarket or grocery store. I should mention at this point that my wife never used Microdyn, opting to just wash fruits and vegetables thoroughly in water, and we got by without incident, so who knows. But still, it doesn't hurt to side with caution, and I am not advising you to chance it.

Eating Out Safely

When eating out, there are also several commonsense measures to follow to keep your tummy happy. First of all, avoid eating at restaurants or getting food from foodstands that are oddly void of customers. Locals know what places are safe and good and which are not. Let their absence from a given establishment stand as a warning message to you.

People also say you should avoid eating lettuce or salad while out as it might not have been properly handled or cleaned, especially since with all its nooks and crannies and crevices, doing so is a tough job. Lettuce, of course, can be a hard thing to avoid, since it comes on things, such as in sandwiches, and on its own, so it is probably best to judge a salad by its seller. If the place has all the signs of being a place that follows good hygiene practices and has an encouraging number of customers, then you should be OK.

Also, avoid the bowls of salsa that are there sitting open on the table all day. Sure, it seems great to have it there in front of you as you nibble your way away, but if that bowl has not been covered or refrigerated while not in use, it could be little cauldron of bacteria looking for a new human home. Yikes.

In this same vein, avoid food stalls with condiments, particularly mayonnaise, sitting out in the sun unrefrigerated. If you learned anything as a kid, it should be that eating a tuna or egg salad sandwich left out in the sun is a sure way to get sick, and that is mostly courtesy of the mayonnaise in it, which is rich in eggs and thus goes bad easily.

Be leary of buying chile rellenos from street vendors, particularly as the day wears on. The chiles are covered in fluffed egg, and the longer eggs sit, the worse they are for you, just as they are in mayonnaise. Let your gut reaction be a guide in protecting your gut.

Finally, just let your instincts be a guide. If a restaurant or street stand look dicey or unclean, stay clear. If a dish looks or even tastes slightly off, don't eat it.

Tap Water - Don't Drink It

You've probably heard it said a million times when talking about visiting Mexico: *Don't drink the water.* Some long-term expats like to boast that they've always drunk the water and have been perfectly fine. Well, all I can say is that if the locals don't drink the water, why would you? People tell you to not drink the water, and we're talking about tap water, because it can make you sick. Sure, some places have fewer problems than others, but still, why chance it?

Almost every apartment, house, school and restaurant, even street food stand, uses filtered bottled water for consumption purposes. You can buy it at the local market or the convenience store, of course, but most people have big bottles, called *garrafones*, of water delivered to their home or place of business. The price is very reasonable too. I mean even if the tap water were safe to drink, the bottled stuff tastes better and is more healthful, which is why many in the US drink bottled water rather than tap water.

Remember that the don't-drink-the-water "rule" is not merely about bacteria. It is also about the possible presence of dangerous chemicals or heavy metals. That all said, just boiling the water is not enough. At any rate, play it safe; drink bottled water. Remember Flint!

Diarrhea

Forgive me for abandoning all the usual euphemisms for this common malady, but people want to know what they need to know, so I figure it is best to be direct in this case. Try as you may to play it safe, it is almost inevitable that you will at some point get the Big D. I mean I've gotten it from eating food from high-end supermarket buffets in the US numerous times, so it is bound to happen, especially in a foreign country where such problems are common enough. Fortunately, help is nearby wherever you happen to be. Almost every OXXO convenience store in the country, whether in a tourist zone with lots of expats or in more purely Mexican areas, seems to have bottles of Pepto Bismol for sale on a rack at the front counter.

If the "Big Pink" has worked for you before, it might just do the trick for familiar feeling occurrences in Mexico. For occurrences that feel less than familiar, i.e., worse than usual, many resort to a medicine called *Kaomycin*, which is a blend of the antibiotic Neomycin, and the chalky substance known as Kaolin, which used to be used in popular anti-diarrheal meds, such as Pepto Bismol and Kaopectate. (By the way, the FDA no longer allows its use, not because of any inherit danger, but because of lack of evidence that it stops diarrhea). You can buy Kaomycin tablets at every pharmacy in Mexico, and many people carry a few around with them whenever they travel just in case the need arises. I've only had one incident in Mexico requiring anything more than the swig of Big Pink (Pepto Bismol), and I can say that the Kaomycin really did the job! Of course, if you have a case of diarrhea that seems much worse or is lasting longer than normal and/or with additional symptoms that are not what you are familiar with, it is best to seek some medical advice. You can start with one of the clinics at your local pharmacy, and if what they suggest does not do the trick, then a visit to the doctor will be in order.

Of course, taking Kaomycin or any other antibiotic does not prevent diarrhea and should not be used for that purpose. By taking it for that purpose, all you do is build up your body's resistance to the antibiotic, which you do not want to do. What you should do instead for prevention is to not drink the water and then follow the food health suggestions made earlier in in the chapter. Many also suggest probiotics, particularly *S.boulardii*, as a way of helping your gut build up a good defenses against travellers diarrhea. S. Boulardii (*saccharomyces boulardii*) can be taken as a supplement in pill form or ingested naturally through the consumption of foods and drinks such as kombucha, mangosteens, lychees, and kefir.

Watch Your Feet

Many Mexican colonial towns have at least some cobblestone streets left. They are quite lovely, but they can be hard on your rump when riding a bike, and, more importantly, dangerous to your ankles should you be wearing the wrong type of shoe. You would be surprised how many women I saw back in Guanajuto who had twisted an ankle while wearing heels on cobblestone. And it is not just heels on cobblestone that one has to watch out for either.

There are all sorts of other things on the ground that can cause you physical grief. On my very first full day in Mexico, Coyoacán to be exact, I was walking along toward Frida Kahlo's Casa Azul, and on the way I suddenly noticed that I was about to be passing in front of the nearby Leon Trotsky Museum. I was looking up and to the left to get a look of the place as I passed, and suddenly, *plop. . . bam. . . splat. . .* I was on the ground, my glasses broken, and some blood was dripping from my knees and the palms of my hands. It turns out that my right foot stepped into a recessed tree planter in the sidewalk, and I thus took quite a stumble.

I would later come to stumble over all sorts of things in the following couple of months, and I would witness similar stumblings by others. The lesson of it all being that one must watch one's feet, or at least what comes before them, while walking about in Mexico, at least if you want to keep your bones in the number of pieces they originally came in.

Stepping Off The Curb

It might sound like an odd thing to mention in this health matters chapter, but you'd be surprised how many people I've met in Mexico, both expat and local, who were hit by a car when stepping off a curb, with the most of those incidents happening in the city of Oaxaca. I am not sure if these incidents happen because of simple negligence or impatience, but they do happen. That said, when stepping out into the street, follow those rules you no doubt learned in elementary school. You know, the basic stuff: look both ways before crossing or even entering the street; cross at the crosswalk, not between cars; avoid wearing dark colors at night; do not assume drivers see or notice you; and don't assume a driver is going to do the right/legal thing.

Yes, OK, I know. That all really does sound like stuff you would tell a kid, but kids in your day probably had it easier when crossing the street, depending, of course, where they grew up. In Mexico, you're talking about big cities, fast traffic, lots of taxis, cars jockeying for a place to park, pedestrians popping out of nowhere, and drivers thus looking in so many directions that they might just miss you if you jump out into the street at the wrong moment. Practicing safety like a kid is better than being locked up in your apartment in casts for months. Pedestrians have the right of way in Mexico, as in most places, but it is probably safer for you to move about as if it is the cars that are king.

Acclimate To The Altitude

One thing people often forget about much of Mexico is that it is, outside of coastal regions, at a higher elevation than the "Mile High City" of Denver, Colorado, as I have mentioned earlier in the book. Many of the spots that expats visit most in Mexico are one or two thousand feet higher than Denver, which is at a relatively measly 5208 feet above sea level. This means that you might suddenly find yourself rather winded after walking up a short flight of stairs or walking up a hill in the first few days at such altitudes, especially if you live in low-lying areas back home. Time usually is the cure for most healthy people. A week or two should do it, but if you are weaker, older and/or at a higher altitude, the acclimation process might take weeks or even months, and for some folks, well, they just never get used to it, which is something to consider when picking a place to live in Mexico.

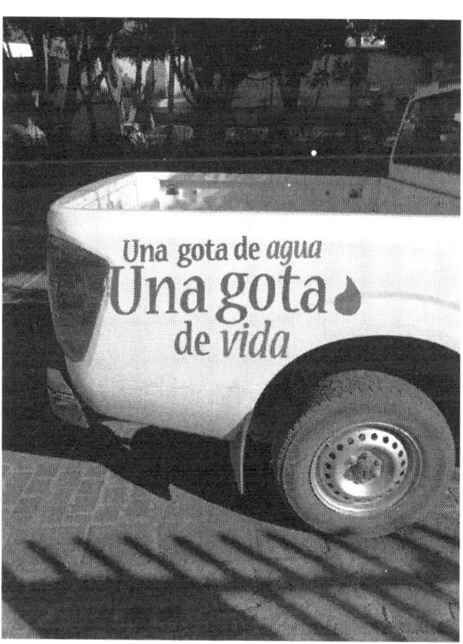

CHAPTER 15: SHOPPING

No matter where you are in the world, you will need at least food and clothing, and that means that you have to shop. Of course, this means that shopping will be a part of your life's activities in Mexico as well, a point that makes some people very, very happy. Fortunately, Mexico has lots of options to offer you for this purpose. I will introduce some of these here, so that you will know what is available to you, what sort of things each carries, and how you go about doing the actual act of shopping at each.

Mercados

Mercados are about as Mexican a shopping experience as you can get. If you are not already familiar with the Mercados in Mexico, they are essentially a collection of independent specialized shops, more like stalls, housed within a larger enclosed space. Most towns have at least one mercado, and in bigger cities, you will find many more, some acting as a sort of anchor for a residential neighborhood.

In most mercados, you will find one or more vegetable vendors, fruit vendors, and separate butchers for different kinds of meat, which means you will find one or more stalls for beef, chicken, pork, and often fish. A good mercado usually has a spice and grains shop, where you can buy spices, rice, beans, and that sort of thing. There might also be bakeries, cheese stalls, candy stalls, and even stalls that sell school supplies and other paper goods. Usually, there is also an area in the mercado that is something akin to a food court, where one can stop and have a good meal made with fresh ingredients at a reasonable price.

In some really large mercados, you will probably find things such as clothes, hats, and even souvenirs. Some even sell pets and tropical fish. At many mercados, you are also likely to find vendors outside as well, often selling flowers, snacks, magazines, and sometimes offering services, such as key making or knife sharpening.

Shopping at a mercado is quite different than at a supermarket. First of all there are no carts, so it is always wise to bring a strong reuseable shopping bag in which to place your acquisitions. The other thing that is different is that you don't touch anything you want to buy. The vendor does the picking up and bagging, though you can point to a particular pear or orange or whatever you want them to bag. Just don't touch. The same is true with meats, though that will will be apparent enough, as there are no packaged cuts of meats to pick up and put in your bag. It is all strictly like trips to butcher in the old days back home where you would just tell the butcher what cut of what meat you wanted and how much of it. Another difference that comes up at mercados is paying. Each vendor stall at a mercado is independent, so you pay for what you want at each stall. There is no central checkout counter.

Shopping at a mercado has its perks. One of which is that the meat, fruits, and vegetables are usually much fresher than what you will find in the supermarkets, usually noticeably fresher. On top of that, the cost of things, especially food, at a Mercado is generally cheaper than at supermarkets and local mom and pop shops. Not only are things cheaper in general, but you can also buy exactly the amount you want and/or need. Want to buy a couple chicken legs for dinner and some chorizo and three eggs for breakfast? You buy exactly that, thus lessening the chance for wasted food.

A downside, particularly for one who doesn't speak Spanish, is that you need to be able to communicate in Spanish, which might prove intimidating for some. Communication, however, means communication, and thus it is not dependent on words alone. You can get away with not being able to speak Spanish, in many cases, as long at you know the numbers in Spanish. Armed with that limited vocabulary set and your index finger, you can do a lot more shopping than you would think. Just go, for example, to the fruit vendor, point to the peaches or apples or whatever it is you want and say the number of items you want. Adding gestures to indicate size or quantity and words like *kilo* or *medio kilo* (half kilo) and the phrases *un poco más* (a little more) and *un poco menos* (a little less), will give you even more buying power.

Remember that these vendors are there to make money, not evaluate your Spanish, so don't worry too much about that side of things. The more you go, the easier it gets. A mercado shopping visit is usually a very lively and interesting thing to do, so by all means at least give it a try.

Supermarkets And Hypermarkets

Food shopping is not restricted to mercados in Mexico, as there are also supermarkets and hypermarkets, just as there are in the United States and Canada. In bigger cities you will find Walmart, Sam's Club and Costco stores as well as their Mexican counterparts, like Bodega Aurrerá. Depending on where you live, you will also most likely have one or more supermarkets like Chedraui, LaComer, Soriana, Superama, Mega, and City Market.

You are no doubt already familiar with hypermarkets like

Walmart, Costco and Sam's Club, so I won't spend time going over those stores other than to say that your Sam's Club and Costco cards will work in Mexico. No need to get a new one. If you aren't already a member of those stores and thus join in Mexico, then you can use your Mexican Sam's Club or Costco card in the US, except for purchases from the Costco.com website.

Jumping over to the topic of supermarkets, not all markets are created equal. They can differ greatly from chain to chain. City Market and LaComer, for example, are truly deluxe stores in every way. I have never seen a supermarket as nice back home as some of the stores in those chains in Mexico. Other stores, such as Soriana, are pretty much on par with what most supermarkets are like back home.

Of course, there are not only differences between supermarket chains, but almost between the branches within the same chain. I remember in Mexico City being so surprised at how the Superama store in posh Polanco was not particularly posh but rather just perfectly adequate, while the one in Condesa was like heaven, with an amazing array of imported cheeses and delicatessen meats, wonderful pastries, and delicious prepared and packaged meals. I loved going to my Superama in Condesa!

At any rate, shopping at a supermarket or hypermarket is pretty much the same as it is back home, so you will have no problems there. And since everything, or just about everything, is packaged, you don't even have to worry about your linguistic abilities. The only blip that ever came up for me, and it was one that took me a long time to figure out, was trying to make out what they were asking me at checkout. Turns out it was pretty much what they often ask you back home, albeit in Spanish: "Do you have a rewards card?" Ha!

One last thing worth noting is that the baggers at the checkout counter who put your groceries into bags are not paid. They work strictly off tips, so it is customary to tip them by handing them any loose coins you are handed back in your change by the cashier. Of course, if the cashier hands you back an unreasonably great number of high denomination coins, you might want to be more selective in how many of them you give.

Mom And Pop Grocery Stores

In addition to the shopping outlets I have mentioned thus far, you will also come across many local neighborhood markets. These mom and pop type places often have most of what you need, and they are pretty much self-serve sorts of places, though some might have a butcher counter inside, where you can specify what you want from whomever is behind the counter. All items are paid for up front at the cashier.

I used to like these little markets mainly because they were easy to use and closeby to where I lived, seldom being more than a block or two away. And because pretty much the same people are working behind the counter every time you go, you do develop a bit of a part-of-the-neighborhood sort of feeling. Prices can be a bit higher, and they don't have the variety you will find at a proper supermarket, but when you are living life as a pedestrian, convenience counts.

Eggs And Chicken

OK, so this might seem an odd section to have here, but there is a good reason for me to mention it, and I will start with eggs. First of all, you will find that eggs are usually not refrigerated in Mexico. If you have lived on a farm or grew up eating farm-fresh eggs, this would not be surprising to you since you probably are used to it. The reason for this state of non-refrigeration is that eggs, all eggs, have a natural protective layer which protects the eggs from the outside world, so to speak. In the US, that coating is washed away during the packaging phase, and thus the eggs must then be refrigerated in order to keep them safe.

The second egg surprise that you will experience is that at mercados and mom and pop stores, the eggs are sold individually. Thus you can buy one or two or whatever number you want. That is handy for someone who doesn't eat eggs that often, like me. The only problem is that they usually put the eggs in a clear plastic bag, and it is then your responsibility to get those eggs home intact. I just took to buying one more egg than I am going to need since I invariably break one by the time I get home.

Moving on to the topic of chicken, we come to another thing that tends to surprise first timers at the mercado when they buy chicken - the chicken is more often than not. . . yellow. Expats can be excused for worrying that the chicken is jaundiced or has been treated or spiced or artificially colored or is somehow sickly or is the result of some weird genetic engineering, but it is not because of any of those things.

Instead, think of what happens to a person when they eat way too many carrots or oranges - the palms of their hands and soles of their feet can turn orange, a temporary and harmless condition known as *Carotenemia.* Likewise, the yellow skin of chicken meat in Mexico occurs naturally because of what the chickens are fed, which is marigold seeds and/or flowers, and as you know, marigolds are yellow or orange, as are their seeds.

Of course, you can usually find the usual pale pinkish chicken at the bigger supermarkets, but after you get used to the yellow chicken, the other stuff looks sort of anemic. Some people say they can taste a difference between the two shades of fowl, but I can't say that I've noticed any difference myself. Still, I did develop a preference for the healthier looking yellow bird. That all said, fear not the yellow chicken!

Tortillerías, Panaderías, And Other Specialty Shops

You can buy tortillas just about everywhere, be it a mercado, supermarket or convenience store. But there are also places that specialize in tortillas. These *tortillerías* are where the tortillas are made, and so if you want your tortillas as fresh as possible, then this is where you need to go. Not only do they sell tortillas, but they also often sell tubs of freshly made Spanish rice and cooked beans, so you could get some of the sides you want to serve with your meal at these stores alone.

Remember that most of central and southern mexico is corn tortilla country, while when you get into the northern states, flour tortillas become increasingly common, and better in quality and taste, so don't go thumbing your nose at flour tortillas while you're up in Chihuhua or Sonora.

More ubiquitous than tortillerías are the the Mexican bakeries, *panaderías*. These stores sell bread, such the *bolillos* used for making tortas, and Mexican sweet bread pastries (*pan dulce*), such as *conchas*, *conchitos* (gingerbread pigs), *empanadas*, *orejas*, and, my favorite, *besos*. Panaderías are self service sorts of places. You enter the store, pick up a tray and pair of tongs, and then load that tray with whatever treats you want. When done, take the tray up to the counter, and they will tally up your purchase and bag it all up for you.

By the way, if you would like a guide to walk you through the world of *pan dulce*, Maura Hernández has a wonderful guide on her site The Other Side of the Tortilla. You can find that guide at the URL below:

> https://theothersideofthetortilla.com/2018/12/guide-mexican-pan-dulce/

There are other specialty shops you will run into that also end with the *-ería* suffix. You will no doubt find *carnecerías* (for meat), *papelerías* (for stationary, school supplies, and the like), *librerías* (bookstore), and so on.

OXXOS And Mom And Pop Tienditas

If you are not familiar with OXXO yet, you certainly will be the minute you leave the confines of whatever airport you land in. In fact, you might find one or two in the airport as well. OXXO is a Mexican convenience store chain that sells all the usual convenience store items: sodas, candy, snacks, dog food, common medicines (Pepto Bismol, Tylenol, etc), packaged baked goods, and sandwiches, and sometimes beer, among other things. Not only can you buy all that, but you can also pay your bills and even buy bus tickets up at the counter. The stores are bright, clean, usually have parking lots, and are generally open 24 hours a day. They are very often packed.

There are expats who don't seem to like OXXO stores, seeing them as putting local mom and pop stores out of business and pushing sugary and fattening junk on the masses. My view is that mom and pop stores sell the same stuff and are not going out of business, so what's the problem? I mean OXXO stores create a lot of jobs, so that is a definite plus. All that said, do what you think is right, but at least give the stores a look so you can be informed. If nothing else, you might need to go to one to pay an electric bill or buy a bus ticket.

Tianguis

To finish up with the brick and mortar side of things, we jump to the topic of *tianguis*, which are a feature of Mexican life that most everyone loves. Basically, tianguis are temporary open air markets. They are not pop-up markets in the American sense because their locations and opening days are regular. And although regular, there are no permanent structures put or left in place. In some places, the tianguis are held in a street or series of streets that are closed off by local authorities for the purpose of holding the tianguis, sometimes in rural areas this happens in front of the local mercado. Sometimes they are held in front of the village church on church grounds. Sometimes they are held in public parks and sometimes on private land.

The tianguis sell all sorts of things. Many have fruits and vegetables, cooked foods to eat, and even clothes, both modern and traditional. Some are specialized, focusing on one specific type of goods, such as organic foods, fresh and cooked dishes, or artisanial goods, such as the mega tianguis in Tonalá, Guadalajara. At any rate, even if you don't buy anything at a tianguis, they are fun events where you can feel the life of the city or village at play.

Amazon.com And Amazon.mx

Finally, you will be glad to know that you can keep making purchases through Amazon once you're in Mexico, and not just from Amazon.com, but also from Amazon.mx. I have bought many things from both, and like other expats, I've have had very good service and no real problems. The only time I've had problems was when I lived on a *privada*, a private street that does not usually appear on maps. I got around that problem by asking the girls at the tiendita near my apartment if they would accept packages for me. They agreed, so I used their shop as the shipping address. All worked out just fine.

CHAPTER 16: CONNECTIVITY

Cell Service, Internet, and Mail

Staying in touch is a major concern to everyone who travels or moves abroad. People not only want to be able to contact family and friends, both old and new, but they also have responsibilities back home that follow them wherever they go. Bills, official letters and more all need to be sent somewhere. Being abroad makes this all a bit more complicated, though not so much so that it should cause you any grief.

Using Your Cell Service Back Home In Mexico

Let's start with cell phone service since this concerns not only future residents but tourists as well. In fact, tourists usually have the easiest time of things because their time abroad is usually limited enough to just stick to their plans back home and add, if it is not already included in their current package, Mexico coverage. This is one of the lucky things about travelling to Mexico - it is close enough to be quite cheap when it comes to extending your current phone service to include it. In fact, it is almost always bundled as a Mexico and Canada package. Such packages give you talk, text, and data in Mexico using Mexican cellular networks, usually Telcel. I have had this add-on service through T-Mobile and Metro PCS (now Metro by T-Mobile), and had absolutely no problems. Most other providers offer the same service.

Many people who move to Mexico for longer periods of time also go this route because it allows them to retain their telephone number back home, which they often want for convenience or business purposes. One problem with this approach is that it is not permanent. All carriers, US carriers at any rate, will eventually terminate your service if it appears clear to them that you are using your service back home for domestic purposes in Mexico, meaning that you are not really using it as a US cellphone in the US. Such people just use that service until that day of reckoning comes.

Mexican Cell Service

Most expats either early on or eventually switch over to a Mexican cell service provider, and there are several, including: AT&T, Virgin Mobile, and the king of them all - Telcel. All of them provide cheaper service than what you would get back home. Some providers are more prevalent than others in certain areas, and in other areas you might not see some at all. No matter where you are, however, you will always find Telcel.

That fact alone is reason to go with Telcel if you are going to switch. And to get Telcel service is easy enough, as you can either buy a phone with the Telcel sim card already in it, or you can just buy the sim and pop it into your phone from back home, though your phone must be *unlocked* in order to go that route. There are different Telcel plans, but the easiest to deal with plans are of the pay-as-you-go variety as they require no contract and have no requirements to deal with. Payment is also easy, as you can just go and pay at a Telcel shop, any OXXO, or any other shops that provide Telcel refill service (copy shops and *papelerías* seem to be common spots offering this service).

Telcel's pay-as-you-go plans come in a variety of different flavors, so to speak, and the one that I cannot recommend any more strongly is the *Amigo Sin Límite 200*. The "200" part of the name refers to the cost, which is $200 MXN a month, which is about $12 US. And for that deal of a price you get all this: 3 gigs of data and unlimited talk and text in Mexico, the US and Canada; unlimited use of of WhatsApp in Mexico, the US, and Canada; and unlimited use of Facebook, Messenger, Instagram, X (formerly known as Twitter, as the press always seems to point out), and Snapchat, though unlimited Snapchat usage is for inside Mexico only.

There are even cheaper Telcel Sin Limite plans, which offer more limited minutes or perks, and there are slightly more expensive ones which give you even more time and perks, so have a look at the TelCel Amigo Sin Limite site to see what you think. Personally, I find the 200 to be perfect, but, it's your phone and your money, so get whichever you think will work best for you.

One thing I should warn you, though, is that when you do go to a shop to "recharge" (*recarga*) your Amigo plan, be sure that you specify "Sin Limite 200." If not, you will most likely be put on the very limited and annoying traditional pay-as-you-go Amigo plan, with which your minutes, for a modern data-heavy user, seem to vanish in a day or two. It is also worth nothing that some shops that offer refill service, can only do so for the traditional pay-as-you-go plans, so be sure to make sure they can refill the Sin Limite plans.

WhatsApp

I figured that while we are on the topic of cell service, I might as well give you a heads up about WhatsApp. In case you're not familiar with WhatsApp, let me start by describing what it is and does (and if you already know, please bear with me). WhatsApp is an application, primarily used on cellphones. It was created back in 2009 as an iPhone app in Mountain View, CA. WhatsApp Inc was an independent company until it was bought by Meta (Yes, Facebooklandia) in 2014. That said, it pretty much does all the things that Facebook Messenger does: text based messages, voice calls, and video calls.

WhatsApp is big around the world, and it is definitely big in Mexico. You will see a store or company's WhatsApp contact info listed with its traditional snail mail, phone, and email contact information on webpages, business cards, and advertisements. Many expats who had no reason to use WhatsApp before, having used other social media apps or just telephone and text instead, start using the app once they move to Mexico so as to better integrate with how things are done there. And, of course, some expats don't, and fair enough. As you spend more and more time in Mexico, you will know whether or not you will benefit by downloading, installing, and using the app.

Internet Service In Mexico

Mexico is a very well connected country Internet wise. Most big cities have excellent high speed networks, and for most apartments, Internet service is included in your rent. Internet service is also included in practically all hotel rooms and AirBnB rentals. While out and about in town, restaurant chains and coffee shops almost always have free Internet service, some requiring a password to connect. Free Internet service is also provided in public buildings, such as libraries and medical facilities, and many public parks also provide free service.

If you happen to rent a place that does not include Internet service, and thus have to get service on your own, check with locals in the same area to see what the local fiber optic cable provider is, and sometime there is more than one, in which case you want to ask around to see which is the best. You can also get Internet access through satellite and via cellular services. Of course, the fiber optic option is usually the fastest, most reliable, and least expensive.

Mail Service In Mexico

Mexico has its own public mail service, *Correos de México*. It does not have a particularly good reputation with people, especially among expats, as people say things too often get lost in the mail. It can also be very slow, especially for international mail. I remember on my first trip to Mexico, I sent four picture post cards (does anyone else do that anymore?). One to Korea, one to Serbia, and two to the United States (Nevada and North Carolina). The cards to Korea and Serbia arrived in one month, while the two sent to the US took two months. Go figure.

I also received a post card from Korea while in Guanjuato, which took two weeks to arrive, and a package (also from Korea) full of snacks and goodies, while in Oaxaca, which took about three weeks to arrive. My wife and I also sent about eight rather hefty boxes from Cuernavaca to northern New Mexico via Correos de México's international express mail service, and it took about a week, which was much faster than we had anticipated. . .or planned for. That all said, our own experiences with Correos de México have not been all that bad.

Still, other expats don't trust it and thus opt to use private shipping services such as UPS or FedEx. Most, in fact, have more confidence in FedEx, and thus tend to use it, when they really want to be sure something is going to get through to its destination. Of course, just as back home, shipping via UPS or FedEx is going to cost you more, so be prepared to be coughing up some American sized payments. Both FedEx and UPS offices can be found around the country.

What About My Mail Back Home?

Wherever you go, you will still have mail back home of some sort that needs to be dealt with. People handle this usually in one of three ways. First, for those who still have a home back home, they just have someone who is staying there or some friend or family nearby check the mail and let them know what has come. Definitely an easy way to go about things, though a bit of an imposition on the mail gatherer in some cases.

Another frequently used method, particularly for those who do not have a home of their own back home anymore, is to do a change of address to a family member's or friend's address. That also works smoothly, though again, it can be a burden on the receivers in some cases.

Finally, a very common way of handling your mail is to have it sent to a private P.O. Box company. There will be a fairly small monthly fee for these services, but there are benefits. These companies will not only collect your mail, but they will also scan the front face of the envelopes, and post the scans online on a page that only you will have access to. There you can see what has come in. If something looks important, you can ask them to open and scan the contents of the mail (for a reasonable additional per-item fee), and if it is something you want sent to you or to someone else, you can ask them to do that for a reasonable fee. You can even set up your account so that they can deposit any checks that come your way into your bank account. Very convenient!

Such companies are found all over the country, so you can ask around for recommendations from other expats to see what they've used and liked. For my part, I have used US Global Mail out of Houston, TX, with great satisfaction.

CHAPTER 17: CAT & DOGS

Many expats move to Mexico with their cats or dogs. Not only are they, to most, like family members, they also provide a lonely expat in a new world with a bit of company and a connection with their life before, thus offering some positive continuity. Others acquire a pet while in Mexico, having either found a need within them for some pet companionship or by having been adopted by a pet.

If you are a dog owner, you acquire additional benefits because your pups need to be walked, and thus you are forced to do something other than shopping, eating, or sightseeing. You are instead out there participating in regular life activities, just like others in the community. Not only are you and your pup getting some exercise, but you are also increasing your interactions, or the chances for interactions, with locals and other expats, particularly those out walking their dogs.

Bringing Your Cats And Dogs To Mexico

If you're bringing your pet to Mexico from the US or Canada, you'll be glad to know that it is a pretty easy thing to do, and, in fact, easier than it used to be just a few years ago. You can bring in two pets per person, and beyond that, you have to pay a duty. Otherwise, you basically don't have to do anything, assuming your pet is a dog or a cat.

All you do is bring your Puff or Spot into the country, where he or she will be briefly inspected at the airport by an agent from OISA (*Oficinas de Inspección de Sanidad Agropecuaria = Agriculture and Livestock Health Inspection Department*) of the SENASICA (*Servicio Nacional de Sanidad, Inocuidad y Calidad Agroalimentaria*), and then you are done. The SENASICA site says it is the same procedure be it at airports or land points of entry, but we have yet to be asked for anything in regard to our pets when crossing the border by land, so don't worry too much about that. Of course, not worrying about something is not the same as not being prepared.

I tend to subscribe to the you-never-know-what-might-happen school of thought, particularly when it comes to Mexico, and it sure paid off when I first flew into Mexico with my cat. According to the USDA APHIS site and that for its Mexican equivalent, I needed various docs, for my pets, but a rabies vaccination certificate was not listed, and so I put all they asked for in a special folder, but I brought a rabies vaccination just in case. I did not include the rabies certificate in the folder I handed in to the OISA inspector because if I learned one thing in my pre-retirement career working with students getting US student visas it is that you never turn in anything that you have not been asked for, just bring it in case you are asked. Sure enough, the OISA agent there at the BJX (León) airport, quickly shuffled though the required docs, and then, with a look of panic in his face, asked where the rabies certificate was. Phew! I pulled it out of my bag, handed it over, and all was hunky dory.

All in all, coming into Mexico with your pets is pretty easy, but, as I said just moments ago, always be prepared for a dose of Murphy's Law to hit at anytime. That said, I personally would not be comfortable entering Mexico, especially at an airport, unless I had a health certificate from the vet, a detailed record of my pets' vaccinations, and a rabies vaccination certificate. And, of course, I would not hand over any of those documents to an agent unless asked.

You can find regulations on bringing your pets to Mexico online from the USDA APHIS in the US or from the Mexican SENASICA.

Flying Into Mexico With Your Dogs And/Or Cats

All this talk about requirements to bring your pet into Mexico has centered on what the Mexican government wants from you. When you fly in, you also have to consider what the airlines want, and what they want often varies from airline to airline, and from the government, so be sure to see what paperwork your airline wants from you before thinking you're all set.

Beyond that, you have two options as to how to fly your pet to Mexico: either in the cabin beneath the seat in front of you or checked in as luggage (meaning, in the cargo hold). Each airline has very clear requirements as to their regulations. First, you have to check up on breed restrictions as pug nose type dogs are often not allowed to travel. Then the size of the carrier is of great importance, especially for in-cabin situations, as it must fit under the seat in front of you, and your pet must fit in it well enough to turn around. Since different airlines use different planes for different runs, the carrier dimensions can vary not only from airline to airline, but also from plane to plane.

There is also a restriction on how many pets can fly in cabin on a flight, and since airlines do not reserve pet space, it is pretty much first come first serve when it comes to getting your pet on the flight, so you want to be sure to be at the airport earlier then normal in case there are more travellers with pets than usual.

There are similar categories of restrictions when it comes to transporting pets in the cargo hold, in which you essentially check your pet in as if you were checking in a suitcase, although the specifics will differ. There are also local temperature restrictions for pets transported in this way all over the world, meaning that the airline will not accept checked pets if the weather is too cold or too hot. This can get tricky if the climate at your departure place is quite different from that at your destination. Check with the requirements for each airline you are going to be flying with. Links to the pet information pages for for most Mexican carriers is provided here: AeroMexico, Volaris, Viva Aerobus, TAR Aerolineas (in cabin), TAR Aerolineas (checked in)..

Veterinarians

Mexico has lots of veterinarians, and some of them are excellent, with good treatments and excellent service. The cost of veterinary care is also less in Mexico than it is in the US, which is why a lot of people opt to get certain procedures done across the border in Mexico.

For example, we got our dog's teeth cleaned at a very nice clinic in Puerto Peñasco (Rocky Point), Sonora, for $120 US, which was much less than the $300 US being asked for just across the border in New Mexico. A friend had cataract surgery done on her dog in Tijuana for $3000 US while back in Calfornia it would have been $8000 US.

Of course, just as with doctors and dentists for humans, always look for a veterinarian or pet clinic with a good reputation. Ask for recommendations and read reviews to get a better idea of places under consideration. Visiting the office is also a good idea too for peace of mind.

Pet Boarding

Just as back home, you will be able to board your pet if need arises. Almost all veterinarian offices offer this service, and in some areas you will also find dedicated pet boarding facilities. Areas with lots of expats will also have expats offering pet sitting services, if you are interested in that sort of approach. Not to cast aspersions on fellow expats, but if you are going to use one of their services, make sure you have recommendations and/or references from people who have actually used that person's services before. I only say that because there are some squirrelly expats here and there who scam their ways around the country. . .and the world, for that matter, doing half-baked jobs or running off with your pets and selling them elsewhere.

Pet Groomers

Again, Mexico has almost all the pet services you would find back home, and pet grooming is another. Most bigger veterinarian clinics and pet shops offer this service, and there are also pet salons in bigger cities, most of which seem to be very good (though they can't seem to resist putting little ribbons in the hair of dogs like poodles, shitzus, and terriers).

In Cuernavaca, we ran into an unusual grooming service that aimed to train teenagers the art of pet grooming. Seemed like nice idea, but the result. . . well, let's put it this way: I asked them to give our toy poodle a trim, not cutting too much hair - and no shaving. Well, imagine my shock when I went to pick our little girl up later that day, only to find her completely shaven save for a curly mushroom shaped dollop of curls on the top of her head. . . with a little red ribbon on it. I didn't think my Spanish was so bad as to be that misunderstood. Haha. Oh well, they tried. As they say in North Carolina, bless their hearts.

Stray Dogs And Animal Rescue Groups

You will see a lot of stray dogs in Mexico. . . a lot of them. In general, they are of no danger to people as they are around them all the time, but dogs being dogs, problems can arise, especially if they get into a pack, so always use caution when you see them, particularly if you are out with your own dog. The fact that there are so many of these dogs helps to explain the presence of so many dog rescue groups, many, but not all, of which are run by expats in expat-rich areas.

Such groups try to rescue, care for, and rehome such dogs, with many offering overseas adoption services. Others focus on spay and neuter services and developing awareness. Most of these groups are happy to take on volunteers, and I have yet to find one such group which does not actively seek donations of food and supplies.

You will no doubt be able to find such an organization in whatever place in Mexico you decide to make home, but here are some around the country to give you some idea as to what is out there and what they do or offer. These include Barb's Dog Rescue in Puerto Peñasco (Rocky Point), The Sula Society in Puerto Vallarta, Los Adoptables in Ensenada, SOS Chapala Dog Rescue in Ajijic, and Amigos de los Animales de Guanajuato in Guanajuato.

CHAPTER 18: CHURCHES

Let me wrap things up with some information on churches. Now for those of you who are not Christian, I certainly don't mean to leave you out. I just don't have experience with other worship opportunities in Mexico. If I did, I would be sure to include such information, and in the future, perhaps when I get some direct suggestions from people, I will. In the meanwhile I will stick with what I do know and share that with those of you who are curious, especially since the question "are there any church services in English in town" does often pop up in online groups and forums.

Roman Catholic

Those of you who are Roman Catholics will in some ways have an easy time of things in Mexico in that it is an overwhelmingly Catholic country, where even the smallest of towns seems to have at least one Catholic church. Of course, almost all of the services will be in Spanish at Catholic churches in Mexico, though in expat-rich areas, you are likely to find a church here and there that offers English or bilingual services at least once a week, so ask around wherever you happen to settle.

Even if there are no English services offered near where you are, you at least can take comfort in the fact that Catholic services are liturgical in nature and thus pretty much standardized. If you are a regular church goer, you pretty much already know the parts of the service, so you can pretty much follow along, save for perhaps the sermon. Of course, Anglican/ Episcopalian and Orthodox services are also liturgical, so the same follow-along-able-ness is also true for them.

Anglican/Episcopalian Churches

Mexico has many Anglican and Episcopalian churches around the country, and many, if not most, of them offer English services. This is due to the fact that many of these churches have large numbers of expats as parishioners. Such churches thus also very often act as a social hub for expat residents and visitors alike, which is why many have at least a few folks in attendance who are not religious at all but enjoy the company and activities.

These parishes are also good places to meet locals because most also have local congregants and/or additional services in Spanish. Mind you, the number of actual expat Anglicans or Episcopalians at these Mexican Anglican and Episcopalian parishes is often in the minority, since many members are from different denominations, coming mainly because of the language familiarity. Still it all works out smoothly enough.

Some of the best known Anglican or Episcopalian parishes in Mexico with services in English are St. Paul's in San Miguel de Allende, St. Andrew's Anglican in Chapala, Christ Church in Mexico City, St. Mark's in Guadalajara, St. Michael and All Angels in Cuernavaca, Anglican Church Puerto Vallarta, St. Luke's in Mérida, and Holy Trinity in Oaxaca. I save Holy Trinity for last because that is where my wife and I used to go, and I just wanted to say that if you happen to be in Oaxaca for Christmas and want to go to a Christmas Eve evening service, Holy Trinity has a really beautiful one - maybe one of the nicest I've ever experienced anywhere.

Of course, there are many other Anglican and Episcopalian parishes in Mexico that do not offer services in English, but, as I said for the Catholic churches, it is easy enough to follow along since the services are liturgical.

Eastern Orthodox Churches

Mexico also has some, though not that many, Eastern Orthodox churches, with many different jurisdictions represented. To the best of my knowledge, all services are in Spanish. Most are in the greater Mexico City area, with the biggest, grandest, and most beautiful (IMHO) of these being St. George's Orthodox Cathedral in the Roma Sur neighborhood of Mexico City. St. George's is a parish in the Antiochian Orthodox Church, thus coming from Arab roots, so its chanting is in that lovely style. Another large Antiochian Orthodox church, is the Cathedral of Ss. Peter and Paul, located in Huixquilucan, just west of Coyoacán. The Greek Orthodox Cathedral of Saint Sophia can be found in nearby Naucalpan, just west of Polanco. Also in Mexico City is the OCA (Orthodox Church in America) cathedral, Ascension Cathedral, located at the east end of the city, near the airport. There is also a Russian Orthodox (ROC) church in Mexico City, The Russian Orthodox Monastery of the Holy Trinity, located just a few blocks north of the Angel of Independence. There are a few others churches in other parts of the country that should turn up in your searches.

Other Christian Churches

There are, of course, also Methodist, Presbyterian, Lutheran, and Baptist churches in Mexico, but the only one I have found that has services in English is Lakeside Presbyterian in Chapala, as does, I believe, Lake Chapala Baptist. That doesn't mean there aren't others, of course.

In addition to the mainstream churches I have mentioned thusfar, there are also many non- or inter-denominational churches that offer either bilingual or English services. As is usually the case, these are usually located in areas with lots of expats. Those that I know of elsewhere are Family of God in Puerto Peñasco, Sonora, as is Union Church in both Mexico City and Monterrey, English Christian Church in Querétaro, and Lighthouse Church in Tulum. Of course, there are lots of others in other parts of the country, so, again, ask around when you have found a place in which to settle.

EPILOGUE

And so we come to the end of this journey together. I certainly hope that it was all worthwhile for you, and more importantly, I hope I encouraged, not discouraged, you in whatever you were hoping to find and ultimately do. I know I've tried to play the realist and pragmatist at times, and that can be sort of a drag, especially when you are looking for words of hope, so forgive me that point if you found me a bit much at times.

If I were to leave off with any tidbits of advice, the first thing would be to plan in advance, travel down, and have a look way before any possible move. I would then tell you to sit back and think, weighing what you would gain by moving to Mexico with what you would lose by leaving home.

In that regard, also ask yourself this question: Can I do the things I really like to do in Mexico? Can you, or would you be making sacrifices, and if you do have to make sacrifices, would you be able to fill the void left in the wake of that sacrifice with something else? If so, what?

Maybe that sounds silly, but if your favorite pastime back home is hanging out at the library, then you had better find a place in Mexico that can fill that bill! Sure, going to museums and concerts is great, but if what you really love doing is something else, make sure museums will fill the void.

Finally, I would say not to burn any bridges. Burning bridges is what gets you stuck. I mean we have a friend who sold her house in the US to live the nomad life in an RV, and a very nice one at that. Now, three years later, she already really regrets having sold her house, especially since she cannot afford a new one anymore given the price of things.

Think of how it has been for you when, for example, you moved or cleaned out the attic. What was the first thing you found yourself needing in the next few weeks? I bet it was one of the things you tossed out a week or so before, right?

That all said, don't go selling houses or cars, tossing out or giving away furniture or pots or pans or family photos or heirlooms until you have been abroad for a few years and are sure it is for you. You can get rid of whatever you want after that, and you'll then have a better idea of what you would really not like to do without.

To wrap things up, I think of the folks with whom I had originally thought I would have ray of hope to share. Yes, I am referring to those folks just trying to get by more cheaply yet happily in life in a more positive environment. Mexico used to fit the bill perfectly, but it just doesn't seem to be the place for such folks anymore, at least for now. If it is any consolation, I can say, however, that there are other countries out there that are more wallet friendly in terms of visa qualification than Mexico.

Remember that for a long time, Costa Rica was the go-to alternative to Mexico for retirees, but the cost of living there increased so much as to make it less attractive to expats looking for the good life at a lower cost. Still, the visas are available, and the amount required to qualify is only $1000 dollars a month from a lifetime pension source, such as Social Security.

And Costa Rica is not the only other Latin American country offering residency visas for retirees. Guatemala only asks for proof of $1000 in pension income a month, Nicaragua, Panama and Peru all also only ask for $1000, while Colombia only wants proof of $850 dollars a month. Belize's $2000 a month requirement used to top the list in terms of cost, but it now seems almost affordable, being only about half of what Mexico is asking for.

For some time now, Ecuador had been the most popular alt-retirement spot in Latin America. The monthly amount required to show for a pensionado visa there had been only $800 for a fairly long time, later dropping down to $400 a year before going back up to $1200 last time I looked. The other points considered to be perks were the fact that the national unit of currency was and still is the US Dollar, thus meaning no worries about exchange rates, and the fact that once you have your residency visa, you qualify for health insurance via the very reasonably priced national health system, IESS, which is supposed to provide excellent care.

Sadly, things have gone sour in Ecuador in recent months, with criminal gangs having a field day of things down there. The Ecuadorian president just declared a national state of emergency on Janurary 9, 2024, after armed gunmen took over a television station in Guayaquil and pushed people around while waving machine guns and hand grenades for all to see during a live broadcast. Needless to say, this might not be the ideal time to think about Ecuador.

There are other spots around the globe people retire to. I often hear the Philippines mentioned as well as Vietnam and Thailand, though, if I recall, the latter two don't really have a long-term retirement visa option. Some mention Portugal or even Serbia.

Of course, not having been to any of those other countries, other than Serbia (which is a very nice place), I cannot recommend or not recommend any of them, but expats do move to those countries, and they seem to enjoy their choices. Given all that, such places might be at least worth checking out if you are really determined to retire or just move abroad.

Well, all that all said, I wish you luck in whatever you find as your path to move forward on. And silly as it seems at first to say, in the words of Mike Brady, famous television architect and good ol' dad of a certain fictional blended TV family, "Wherever you go, there you are."

ABOUT THE AUTHOR

Nicholas Grant

Nicholas Grant has been interested in Mexico ever since he was a child living in East Los Angeles, where he would watch the Mexican Indpendence Day parade every year with his grandmother and sup on her delicious cooking, especially her tamales - Matzalán style! Later he would travel to Mexico itself, starting with his first trip to Tijuana with his mom at the age of eleven. As an adult, he would go on to travel, camp, and live in various parts of mainland Mexico.

Prior to a slightly early retirement, Nicholas worked as a K-12 ESL teacher and later as a university study abroad and international student advisor, in which role he also served as the university's SEVIS Primary Designated School Official, responsible for immigration documentation and compliance matters for incoming students from abroad, a role that helped him later on when it came to dealing with the ins and outs of Mexican immigration matters.

When not travelling or camping with his wife, Marie, Nicholas likes to spend time with his dogs, Penny and Elspeth, strum Michael Nesmith and Ian Tyson tunes on his Fender Mustang, and play the Swedish Viking era game of Kubb.

Made in the USA
Columbia, SC
30 April 2025

57359794R00093